The Unofficial Biography of
LIVERPOOL

FourFourTwo

The Unofficial Biography of
LIVERPOOL

DAVID PROLE

PAN BOOKS

First published 1996 by Pan Books
an imprint of Macmillan Publishers Ltd
25 Eccleston Place
London SW1W 9NF
and Basingstoke

Associated companies throughout the world

ISBN 0 330 34974 0

9 8 7 6 5 4 3 2 1

A CIP catalogue record for this book is available from
the British Library.

Phototypeset by Intype London Ltd
Printed by Mackays of Chatham plc, Chatham, Kent

Contents

Foreword

This book, as the title implies, is by no means an official Liverpool FC publication. I have written it from my personal viewpoint, as a follower of the club for half a century.

I started as a supporter, then was a journalist on Merseyside for several years, and for part of that time I had the privilege of reporting Liverpool matches from Anfield and from other soccer strongholds such as Scunthorpe and Rotherham.

Later on I worked in various other places, while still supporting the Reds in mind and body. I still do, but no longer have any contact with the club. For many years now, if I have wanted to see the team play, I have paid to go in. This, I believe, entitles me to have an occasional moan in between bestowing a lot of praise.

A book like this needs a lot of research, and the work of others has been most helpful – particularly *Liverpool, A Complete Record*, by Brian Pead, which proved absolutely invaluable. Stephen F. Kelly's prolific output of Anfield-based books also came in useful, as did the two Liverpool Pocket Annuals so far produced by Words on Sport, and various *News of the World* annuals and Rothman's yearbooks. Certain bound copies of the *Echo* and *Daily Post* were required reading, and I am grateful to the staff at the British Museum Newspaper Library for their assistance. I also did considerable research the modern way, by watching various videos.

I am indebted to Mike Langley, Keir Radnedge, John Kelly and James Georgiou for their help with various matters, and – as ever – to my wife Iris, for her patience and encouragement.

David Prole
August 1996

Chapter One
The growth of a dynasty

In September 1982 I was in Spain on a holiday which included a two-day trip from Barcelona to Andorra. On the way I got into conversation with a young couple from Merseyside and before long the subject moved round to football. The young man, whose name unfortunately escapes me, suddenly said: 'My father-in-law's gorra bewk about Liverpool. It's called *Come On The Reds* and it's great. Have you read it?' With due (I hope) modesty, I had to admit that not only had I read it, I had written it. He took some convincing, to the point when I had to produce my passport in order to prove my identity. He then went along the coach telling other passengers: 'That feller there . . . he writes bewks.' Much conversation and a few beverages followed. Next day, when we got back to Barcelona and went our separate ways, he left with this parting shot: 'I still don't believe it. Fancy meeting the author of my favourite bewk. Before this I'd never met anybody who could write.'

Come On The Reds had been published in 1967. Liverpool had won the League Championship in 1964 and 1966, with the FA Cup in 1965 as the meat in the sandwich. I decided that this unusual feat was worthy of a permanent record so I wrote the book, which eventually turned into a history of the club. This, to my knowledge, was the first such book to appear. It cost a guinea and now costs rather more than that – if you can find a copy. And I like to think that it paved the way for the many other books about the club that have followed.

The preface paid due tribute to the club's successes, as follows: 'Only Arsenal and Manchester United can match the record of seven First Division Championships, supplemented by four in the Second Division. The FA Cup was a different story, year after year ending in frustration, but 1965 surely made up for all which had gone before. European football . . . has drawn some of Liverpool's best performances: no complete victory, but a semi-final in one tournament, a final in another.' Things have changed a bit since then. The total of First Division titles has gone up from seven to eighteen. The solitary FA Cup victory has increased to five. The European scoreboard now lists six victories, the first two in the Uefa Cup and the other four in the Champions Cup. The League Cup, ignored by Liverpool in its early days (until the final was switched to Wembley and offered a new gateway to Europe), has been won a record five times in its various guises. Liverpool's performances have been remarkable, particularly in the twenty-year spell from 1971 to 1991 when the club's positions in the League table were: third, first, second, second, first, first, second, first, first, fifth, first, first, first, second, first, second, first, second, first, second. Thirteen major knockout competitions were won as well. Can any club, in any major footballing country, have a record to compare with that?

Since *Come On The Reds* first appeared, football has changed enormously – not for the better, I submit, m'lud – and Liverpool FC have changed with it. The ground is now barely recognisable from the days when I used to thrill to the sight of Billy Liddell and Albert Stubbins. The old Kop, the most famous single soccer structure in Britain (if not the world), has become a new all-seater architectural triumph – which lacks the old atmosphere. The players are a bit slimmer and a lot faster. Tactics have altered, shirt numbers have gone crazy. The team is now made up of multi-purpose all-rounders with (goalkeeper apart) a variety of jobs to do. 'Twas not thus, before: I remember an end-of-season game when Ray Lambert, a Welsh full-back with a shiny skull, suddenly appeared in the opposing penalty area for perhaps the first time in a lengthy career, and shot narrowly wide. As the Kop played their familiar game of not giving the ball back, a voice was heard crying, in rhyme: 'Eh, Ray, are yer playin' away?' The old uniform, first red with white shorts, then all red ('Makes them look like giants,' said Bill Shankly), is now a fashion accessory for fans and frequently changes to help the scallies stay *à la mode* and to help the club to meet the never-ending bills. Transfer fees have soared into the stratosphere. So have players' wages. The car park is stuffed with the latest metal monsters. The programme is like a phone book. Evidence of sponsorship is everywhere.

The city of Liverpool has altered too: a mixture of new roads and empty shops has sprung up, with an appalling increase in major crime and petty vandalism. The industries that made the port area a boom town of its own have followed the cotton and slave trades into limbo, along with the dockers' umbrella (properly known as the overhead railway), with some compensation in the shape of the splendid Albert Dock redevelopment. All so different, I suppose, from the days, over a century ago, when the lads who had founded Everton, at Anfield, upped and went to a new home, leaving other members of the club behind to start their own. The dispute, not the first in the city to arise because of alcohol, came about because there were no changing rooms at the ground and the players used the nearby Sandon pub. Some felt that this was a bad thing and likely to interfere with their fitness. That, and the chance to buy the land on which Goodison Park was erected, resulted in a split. Those who went took the Everton title with them. Those who stayed adopted their city's name.

Liverpool, the club, are one of the few in England to have had only one home throughout their existence. Liverpool, the city, is the only one to have had at least one club in the First Division ever since the League's foundation in 1888. John McKenna, once a grocer's delivery boy, became a major figure at Anfield, on the committee and then on the board. He was largely responsible for building the team, signing several Scots keen to get their hands on the money that the new professionalism was providing. Everton had been founder members of the Football League: Liverpool followed them in 1893, after winning the Lancashire League title the previous season, the club's first in competitive soccer. The team for the opening match comprised ten Scots and a Lancashire-born goalkeeper named McOwen.

Liverpool started League life as they meant to go on, winning the Second Division title with twenty-two victories and six draws in their twenty-eight games. They also won a Test match to decide promotion and began the next season in Division One with two draws, before their first defeat stopped a run of thirty-one successive unbeaten matches – a record not surpassed until Nottingham Forest's forty-two-game sequence in 1978, which was ended at Anfield. Between then and 1905 Liverpool were relegated from the First Division twice but won promotion at the first attempt both times and remained unbeaten at Anfield. Indeed Liverpool did not lose at home in Division Two until 1954, after forty-eight matches. In 1906 they were League champions for the first time despite losing ten of their thirty-eight games, with a team built around the Scottish international half-back Alex Raisbeck and well served on the right wing by Arthur Goddard; who played 415 matches in thirteen seasons. Three years later they were second, after a remarkable 6–5 win over Newcastle, and in 1914 they reached their first FA Cup final, losing to Burnley by the only goal of the match, scored by a former Everton forward, Bert Freeman.

League football continued long after the First World War broke out, and conflict had been of the killing and maiming variety for almost a year before Liverpool were involved in the infamous 'fixed' match with Manchester United. The result was arranged for betting purposes – United were to win 2–0, and did so after missing a penalty and several other chances – but the fraud was so palpable that it could not hope to succeed. Four players from each side were suspended for life, although these bans were reduced in a post-war amnesty. In another more palatable gesture of solidarity, Liverpool's last match, a 2–0 win at Oldham, ensured that Everton finished champions.

There was a considerable amount of soccer played to entertain the masses while the long war dragged to its conclusion. After it was over, Liverpool suddenly emerged as a leading club and in the first four post-war seasons they were fourth twice and first twice, losing only thirty-five games out of 168 in the newly extended top division. Several of the team, notably goalkeeper Elisha Scott, were internationals. Suddenly, however, standards dropped and the club became stuck in a rut, rarely in danger of relegation but equally rarely looking like potential champions or Cup winners, although they had some excellent players between then and the start of the Second World War. By coincidence, two of these players were forwards bought for big fees (big for that period) after scoring heavily elsewhere, whose playing days soon were ended by injury. In those days a damaged cartilage could mean an early finish to a career. Bill Hartill had scored 164 goals in 221 matches for Wolves, but managed only five appearances for Liverpool. Ted Harston, who had scored fifty-five goals in one season for Mansfield, also played a mere five times. These two followed a notable striker of the early days, Joe Hewitt, and were contemporaries of 240-goal Gordon Hodgson and Fred Howe (who once scored four in a game against Everton) and preceded other post-war 'Hs' such as Hickson, Hunt, Hateley and Heighway.

Nearly all the players immediately went into the forces in 1939 (many had been in the Territorial Army in preparation), travelling back to play whenever they could. Guest players were common and the fixtures, bizarre though some of them were, did a great deal for morale in those difficult days. Eventually the game got going again and the players gradually returned. Two of them, Bill Jones and Eddie Spicer, had been decorated for bravery; Spicer, serving in the Marines, captured a German paratrooper who turned out to be a professional footballer, and an international at that.

With several veterans left from pre-war days and some younger players coming through, including Liddell, Paisley and Stubbins, signed from Newcastle for a club record £13,000, Liverpool proved strong enough to win the Championship in the first post-war season, which lasted from August 1946 to the following June. An appalling winter (twenty-two miles of the A1 in Yorkshire were blocked for several days) and fuel shortages, combined with a ban on midweek matches as part of the effort to get the country back into recovery mode, led to this marathon. Liverpool had a fortnight to wait after completing their programme. If Stoke could win away to Sheffield United, the title was theirs on goal average. They lost, and the scenes at Anfield; where a local derby was being staged in the Liverpool Senior Cup; were something extraordinary, although they were repeated often in later years.

I was a boy of thirteen at the time, but a regular attendee with my father, in his capacity as *Echo* sports editor. And here I pay tribute to an underrated manager, who did a great deal for the club: George Kay. You do not hear his name mentioned very often, but Liverpool would have been poorer without him. Kay played centre-half for Bolton, Belfast Celtic and West Ham, and was captain of the Hammers – against Bolton – in the first Wembley FA Cup final in 1923. He later managed Luton and Southampton before joining Liverpool in 1936 and, although the board rarely made much money available, he did well as a buyer. He wanted Matt Busby to become a full-time coach after the war. He pioneered tours abroad, to the USA, Sweden and France, believing that the experience would be good for the team as well as giving them the sort of holiday they could not afford on their restricted wages. He worked night and day on Liverpool's behalf and, as one of nature's worriers, he sadly helped to dig his own grave. Kay could be gruff and ill-tempered but was kind and polite to me, when he had no real need to be, and I remember him with much affection. He died a few weeks before Liverpool at last achieved his big ambition: to win the FA Cup.

At the time of Kay's death Liverpool had had only six managers in their seventy-three-year existence. The first, from 1892 to 1896, was William Barclay, who was a combined secretary-cum-manager and general assistant to the autocratic McKenna, as well as being a school headmaster. He was followed by Tom Watson, formerly of Sunderland, who held the job for nineteen years, with considerable success, until his sudden death. David Ashworth then arrived from Oldham but after three years he unexpectedly returned to his former club, even though Liverpool were on course for the Championship, which they duly achieved. Matt McQueen took over, extending an unusual career in yet another direction. He had been a player, appearing in Liverpool's first League game in 1892 and staying for eight years, then became a qualified League referee, and eventually he was made a director of his old club. On Ashworth's departure McQueen was persuaded to become manager but four years later he lost a leg in a road accident while on his way back from a scouting mission and he resigned soon afterwards. He then had sixteen years in retirement, living in Kemlyn Road adjoining the ground, before his death in 1944. George Patterson, who had been secretary since 1908, now combined that with the job of manager until Kay arrived. Patterson then switched back to his original job but soon resigned due to ill health and was succeeded as secretary by Jack Rouse and Jimmy McInnes until Peter Robinson came from Brighton in 1965.

Kay's successor as manager was Don Welsh, a former
England inside-forward who had captained Charlton
in both the 1946 and 1947 FA Cup finals, losing the
first and winning the second. He had been a guest
player with Liverpool during the war, scoring six goals
in a 12–1 win over Southport, and was a charming and
affable man. Unfortunately, Welsh was not a very good
manager. He could do little to stem the slide towards
the inevitable relegation in 1954 (apparently he went
into the silent dressing room after the match that sealed
the club's doom, after forty-nine seasons in the First
Division, and told the players: 'What a ******* day –
the reserves lost as well!') and in 1956 he became the
first of the club's managers to be sacked. He later
managed Bournemouth, then took over a pub in
Devon, and worked for a time in a hostel for children.
Phil Taylor was perhaps even more affable and charming than Welsh. He joined Liverpool in 1935, from
Bristol Rovers, and never lost his Bristol burr. Taylor
had been a clever if one-paced wing-half, captain at
Wembley in 1950, and had won three England caps.
He was chief coach under Welsh, and after a lengthy
period when his title was merely that of assistant manager, the assistant was lost and the job was his. He had
it for just over two seasons, got near but not near
enough in the promotion chase, and decided to retire
before the strain began to tell too strongly. So Shankly
arrived, and the boom began.

Liverpool fans frequently have made the news in the
past thirty years; but hero worship did not start with
Shankly. Many of the people I worked with in Liver-

pool over forty years ago were stark raving Anfield daft, even in times when titles were few and far between and Wembley could have been Wollongong for all the chance the team had of getting there. When I was on national service a friend who was a Linotype operator would write to me every week, using his tea-break to set his letter in type. He would then send me a proof of it, and without fail there would be paragraph after paragraph about the previous Saturday's match.

When Liverpool at last, at long, long last, smashed the old FA Cup hoodoo and won at Wembley in 1965, their first goal was greeted by a none-too-young fan who got on to the pitch (I do not encourage that sort of behaviour but I was willing to make allowances in this case). He was carrying a rattle, one of those old heavy wooden noise-makers that never would be allowed in a ground now, even if you could find one, because they would be classed as an offensive weapon. A policeman fell on him, followed by two more, and then another two, one of them an inspector. They all clutched various pieces of him and carried him away for ejection. As they did, somehow he managed to thrust an arm in between the acreage of blue serge and whirl the rattle with all his might. For days afterwards, the opening conversational gambit was not the match, or the incredible turn-out of fans when the team took the Cup from station to town hall, but: 'Eh, did yer see that feller carrying those five coppers off?' 'That feller' epitomised the heart and soul of Scouse football humour. By now, I expect, he is no more, but I would not be at all surprised if his family had joined the hundreds of others who ask permission to scatter ashes at Anfield. Rogan Taylor's book, *Three Sides of the Mersey*, carries a dedication from a girl who wrote regarding her late step-father: 'My mum has been to the chapel of rest and put all his football stuff on him so he looks like he's on his way to Wembley.' The wish of all expiring Koppites.

Unfortunately the behaviour of supporters is not always so creditable. I am convinced that Anfield's atmosphere is not what it was and that the same applies on away trips. At Wembley in 1989, as only one example, I was horrified when fans in their hundreds invaded the pitch at the end, even though they were bent on no mischief worse than planting a kiss or two on the players. The Hillsborough disaster was only a few weeks old, and the presence of intruders was far too bleak a reminder.

Liverpool, club and city, were unlucky to be stigmatised widely after Hillsborough. I was not there, thank God, but from conversations, reading and television I am now convinced that the tragedy could have been averted if the crowd had been packed in properly. The central area at the Leppings Lane end was overfull long before the start, while the areas to each side had room to spare. Of course the last-minute surge of fans was a major cause of the crushing, but a last-minute surge is usual at all major events drawing crowds – concerts, theatre, ballet, as well as football – especially when those crowds have had a long journey to the venue. And there seems little doubt that the unfortunate police at first reacted by thinking 'soccer hooligans' rather than 'potential disaster'. This awful tragedy brought out the best in a lot of people, as tragedies tend to do. The players and staff were nothing less than heroic in their determination to offer what succour they could to the bereaved, who of course numbered far more than those who went to a game of football and did not come back. The tributes, floral and tribal, at Anfield were heartbreaking in their poignancy. Part of the city died. And in Milan, before a European match with Real Madrid, fans stood in silence and then sang *You'll Never Walk Alone*, for Liverpool as well as for their rivals from Turin who had died at Heysel four years earlier. Then, the story had been different. Just as most Liverpool supporters should not be heavily blamed for Sheffield, so some cannot be blamed heavily enough for Brussels. True, the stadium was ramshackle by modern standards and ticket allocation was chaotic. True, the Belgian police were unprepared to a remarkable degree. True, there was some provocation from some Juventus fans. But if no Liverpool followers had charged into the Italian section, if the temptation to pick up bits of rubble and throw them had been resisted, if their general desire to show that 'Scousers are better than wops' had been ignored, the deaths would not have happened. That is a stigma that will never go away and it is a stigma that, I believe, has diluted the old affection for Liverpool FC to some extent.

So too has money's elevation to a point far higher than any other in the soccer sphere. I am not alone in feeling some revulsion at the obscene transfer fees, salaries and bonuses now being paid. Liverpool naturally make the most of their purchasing power provided by so many willing payers, while the old Football League creed of fair shares for all now has been abandoned in favour of giving every possible advantage to the wealthy, but that is not the club's fault: they alone cannot influence the other clubs, and they can hardly be blamed if they make the most of what their success has brought them. But there is now a kind of moral bankruptcy about football that stems from the amount of money washing about in what is still laughably called a game; a game that leads a manager such as George Graham to plead that he had done nothing wrong in accepting illicit payments from an agent, that leads the FA to give the England job to Terry Venables, a man described by one writer as making more court appearances than the Old Bailey cat.

Fortunately Liverpool's organisation and tradition is such that little dirty linen leaves Anfield for the public wash-house, although there are a few distressing examples and one more will be one too many. The good side of the club is light years ahead of the bad. Between the early 1960s and the very late 1980s, Liverpool had more success than any other English club in history. The honours had piled up to such an extent that they tended to be taken for granted (have you ever *seen* the trophy room?). Four remarkably successful managers – Shankly, Paisley, Fagan and Dalglish – moulded the talents of many remarkably successful players, from Yeats, St John, Callaghan, Smith and Hunt through Clemence, McDermott, Keegan,

Heighway, the Thompsons and the Kennedys, Hansen and Whelan, Rushie and Brucie and the incomparable Kenny, to Barnes and to Beardsley, to Fowler and McManaman and Redknapp and so many, many more. All have helped to give hope to many who have little else in life but the game at large and Liverpool Football Club in particular. All have contributed an enormous amount to the entertainment of millions, abroad as well as at home.

Hopefully we shall keep alive the memories of all these exponents of a game that is the art of the masses, while the memories of disasters and scandals fade. Hopefully.

1892	Club founded by members who stay put when others quit to form a separate club, Everton.
1893	Champions of the Lancashire League at the first attempt, and elected to Football League.
1894	Unbeaten champions of the Second Division, at the first attempt.
1895	Bottom of the First Division.
1896	Champions of the Second Division with 106 goals – still the club record – in only thirty matches. George Allan scores twenty-five in twenty appearances.
1899	Second in the First Division, losing final match 0–5 to champions Aston Villa.
1900	Lose first eight games but finish tenth.
1903	Sam Raybould is highest scorer in the League

	with thirty-one goals in thirty-three games, a club record until 1931.
1904	Relegated after losing 2–5 to Everton.
1905	Promoted at the first attempt, beaten only three times out of thirty-four.
1906	First Division champions and FA Cup semi-finalists, losing to eventual winners Everton. Kop built.
1910	Second in the table, with Jack Parkinson scoring thirty goals in thirty-one matches.
1914	First FA Cup final, losing 0–1 to Burnley at Crystal Palace.
1915	'Fixed' 0–2 defeat by Manchester United: four players from each club suspended for life (later reduced).
1922	Champions with fifty-one points, thanks mainly to Scott-Longworth-McKinlay defence.
1923	Championship retained with fifty-seven points.
1928	New Kop (with roof) opened by club founder John McKenna.
1930	'Tiny' Bradshaw, one of Scotland's Wembley wizards (his only cap), signed from Bury for club record £8,000. Worst-ever home defeat, 0–6 to Sunderland.
1931	Gordon Hodgson scores thirty-six goals in forty matches, but the team finish only ninth. Elisha Scott plays his 467th and last game, a total later passed by twelve others.
1935	Record defeat to date, 0–8 at Huddersfield.

1939   War stops 'proper' football for six years: Liverpool had finished in top ten only twice in the previous ten seasons.

1947   Champions by a point in first post-war season, winning seven and drawing one of last eight matches, five of them away.

1949   Draw 1–1 with Everton in front of Goodison's highest gate: 78,299.

1950   Unbeaten in first nineteen games (then League record). First Wembley appearance, losing 0–2 to Arsenal.

1952   Anfield's record gate: 61,905 for 2–1 Cup tie win over Wolves. Draw nineteen games, then a League record.

1953   Lose 0–1 to Third Division Gateshead in the Cup, and just avoid relegation.

1954   Down at last, after forty-nine seasons in top division and a club worst of fourteen successive games without a win.

1955   John Evans scores five v. Bristol Rovers. Beat Everton 4–0 at Goodison in FA Cup, six weeks after record defeat, 1–9, at Birmingham in the League. Finish eleventh, lowest position ever.

1957   Third for second year running. Lose 1–2 at Southend in FA Cup.

1959   Fourth for second year running. Lose 1–2 at non-League Worcester in FA Cup.

1960   Shankly becomes manager: finish third.

1961   Third again. Liddell retires after 537 games and 229 goals.

1962   St John and Yeats signed. Second Division champions, scoring ninety-nine goals (Hunt forty-one).

1963   Lose 0–1 to Leicester in FA Cup semi-final, finish eighth after looking possible champions at Easter.

1964   Champions with three games to spare, demolishing Arsenal 5–0 in Anfield clincher. Beaten 1–2 at home by Swansea in FA Cup sixth round.

1965   First FA Cup victory, 2–1 v. Leeds, despite Byrne's broken collarbone, and semi-finalists in first venture into Europe, controversially eliminated by Inter Milan.

1966   Champions again, using only fourteen players in forty-two League games. Also reach Cup Winners' Cup final, losing 1–2 to Borussia Dortmund. Hunt plays all six games as England win World Cup.

1967   Fifth, which is to be their lowest placing until 1992.

1968   Third, beaten in FA Cup quarter-final. Enter League Cup for the first time, losing to Bolton in round two.

1969   Second despite losing only once at home.

1970   Fifth, and beaten by Watford in FA Cup sixth round. Hunt transferred to Bolton after 285 goals in 489 appearances.

1971   Newcomers Toshack and Heighway lead a run to FA Cup final where Arsenal win 2–1 in extra time.

1972   Keegan arrives to become an instant hero, but title goes to Derby in a desperate finish.

1973   Duke of Kent opens new stand and Liverpool celebrate by winning the Championship and the Uefa Cup, beating Borussia Mönchengladbach 3–2 on aggregate.

1974   Shankly retires after 3–0 victory over Newcastle brings second FA Cup success. Second in table behind Leeds. Record win, 11–0, v. Stromsgodset Drammen in Cup Winners' Cup.

1975   Second again, under Paisley.

1976   Title won with 3–1 victory at Wolves in final match, followed by a second Uefa Cup, beating Bruges 4–3 over two legs.

1977   Almost a treble: League again and first of four European Champions Cup triumphs, 3–1 against Mönchengladbach in Rome, four days after 1–2 defeat by Manchester United in FA Cup final. Keegan goes to Hamburg, replaced by Dalglish from Celtic.

1978   Souness signed from Middlesbrough in time to help retain European Cup, 1–0 v. Bruges at Wembley. Second to Forest twice, in League and in replayed League Cup final.

1979   First again with two League records: sixty-eight points and only sixteen goals conceded (four at home). FA Cup semi-final.

1980   Championship retained to compensate for defeats in two semi-finals: Arsenal after three

FA Cup replays, Forest after one League Cup replay. Rush signed from Chester.

1981   Two more trophies: League Cup for the first time, 2–1 in replay v. West Ham, and European Cup, 1–0 v. Real Madrid. Defeat by bottom club Leicester in January is first loss at Anfield after eight-five games unbeaten in all competitions.

1982   Three points for a win introduced. Liverpool total eighty-seven to regain title, and keep League Cup by beating Spurs 3–1 in extra time.

1983   Title retained with eighty-seven points, eleven more than needed, despite taking only two from last seven games. League Cup won for third time in succession, all after being 0–1 down: this time 2–1 v. Manchester United.

1984   Fagan succeeds Paisley and wins three trophies in his first season: the League Cup in a replay against Everton, the Championship by three points and the European Cup in a shoot-out against Roma after a 1–1 draw.

1985   Season ends in tragedy. After second place in League and an FA Cup semi-final replay defeat by Manchester United there is the 0–1 defeat by Juventus in the riot-ruined European Cup final in Brussels, probably soccer's most pointless statistic. Fagan resigns in tears and Dalglish becomes player-manager.

1986   A marvellous first season in charge for Dal-
       glish, despite the ban from Europe. He
       scores the goal at Chelsea that settles the
       title, and a week later helps his team to come
       from behind to beat Everton 3–1 in the FA
       Cup final.

1987   A 13–2 aggregate win over Fulham is a
       League Cup record but there are no trophies,
       only a 1–2 defeat by Arsenal in the League
       Cup Final. This is the first time in the 140
       games in which Rush has scored for Liver-
       pool that he finishes on the losing side (118
       wins and twenty-one draws). Second in the
       League, nine points behind Everton.

1988   Rush goes, Beardsley and Barnes arrive. Ald-
       ridge scores in a club record ten successive
       League games. The first twenty-nine games
       pass without defeat, equalling the League
       best, and the Championship is a formality.
       But Wimbledon bring off an FA Cup shock
       at Wembley.

1989   Hillsborough overshadows all, even the
       remarkable end to the season. Rush, back
       from Italy, scores twice as Liverpool beat
       Everton 3–2 in extra time to win the FA
       Cup, but then lose 0–2 at home to Arsenal
       to miss the League on goal difference.

1990   Eighteenth Championship and a club record
       First Division victory 9–0 v. Crystal Place . . .
       who gain 4–3 revenge in the FA Cup semi-
       final.

1991   Dalglish resigns after the 4–4 FA Cup draw with Everton, who win the replay 1–0. Graeme Souness arrives in April and the club finish second.

1992   The club's centenary year is marked by a return to Europe in the Uefa Cup, but there is a quarter-final exit with two defeats by Genoa. A fifth FA Cup final victory, 2–0 against Sunderland, despite Souness's heart surgery, is some consolation for a slip to sixth in the table and for having six players sent off.

1993   The Queen visits Anfield and meets players and staff. Sixth in the first season of the new Premiership, but there is much disquiet over Souness. Two defeats by Spartak Moscow in Europe and a home crash to Bolton in the FA Cup precede the rebuilding of an all-seated Kop.

1994   Fowler scores all five v. Fulham in a League Cup game but Anfield is in turmoil and in January, after a home Cup defeat by Bristol City, Souness resigns. Evans is promoted from assistant manager. Final position, eighth, is the lowest since 1963.

1995   A rise to fourth and a record fifth League Cup victory; 2–1 over Bolton, followed by Collymore's signing for a British record fee, £8.5m.

1996   Uefa Cup defeat by Brondby. Rush scores in a 7–0 win over Rochdale; breaking the twentieth-century FA Cup record held by Denis Law. It's Rush's forty-first goal in the competition and his 335th for the club. Third in the table, FA Cup final defeat by Manchester United.

Chapter Two
Worth a goal start – The Kop

Anfield contains perhaps the biggest shrine of any sporting arena. The rebuilt Spion Kop, stretching along one end of the ground in all its glory, came about as a direct result of the Hillsborough disaster of 1989. Anfield has a pristine tablet listing the names of all those who failed to survive that awful day, and the Shankly Gates down at the other end are a tribute to a great manager, but Spion Kop is the real memorial.

Ironic that the new Kop is now there as a splendid all-seater in remembrance of so many dead: Anfield's original Kop was named to honour the passing of an even greater number of souls. In 1906, Liverpool FC wanted to erect a new structure to replace the old ash-and-clinker banking that had stood since the early days of the ground, in the 1880s. While they were at it, they decided to engage the celebrated architect Archibald Leitch – known for his designs of various sports arenas, including Goodison Park – to rebuild the entire ground, complete with covered grandstand. Many sons of Liverpool and other parts of Lancashire had perished during the Boer War, and the club called the new banked-up area Spion Kop, after one of the battles in the South African campaign during which the British took a hilltop site in Natal; the next day the reinforced Boers took it back, killing all 297 defenders. The suggestion for the name had come from Ernest Edwards, sports editor of the *Liverpool Echo*, who stayed in that onerous post until 1938, when he was succeeded by my father. (In those self-effacing days writers nearly always were known by pseudonyms. Ernie Edwards was Bee, after his initials, and my dad was known as Ranger. Bee's son Leslie was called Contact, and in due course he too became the *Echo*'s sports editor.)

Spion Kop grew in popularity as the years passed. Crush barriers were installed at various points, and more and more were needed as the Kop became a cheap-to-enter meeting-place for working-class clientele. In 1928 a roof was added, with the rebuilt structure being officially opened by John McKenna, former secretary, director and chairman of the club, and president of the Football League for a quarter of a century. (They later erected a memorial plaque to him, too.)

Some of the *Liverpool Echo* sports staff spent many happy hours at the modified Anfield, and some not so happy hours as they tried to keep in touch with the office despite the vagaries of the telephone system. The modern area housing the media facilities at Anfield is first-class: indeed the entire ground now bears little relation to the old stadium, and is a credit to the architects, the builders and the club, particularly those directors responsible for overseeing the construction.

Whether all this would have happened but for Hillsborough and Lord Justice Taylor's report into ground safety, which followed the earlier disaster at Heysel Stadium in Brussels, is questionable. The fans, in the main, were content to cram into the Kop, which had progressed to an eminence unique in football. Lots of grounds have a kop, but there was only one 'real' Kop, which could accommodate 24,000 standees in an area almost one hundred yards in length and twenty-seven yards deep. To see it on a Saturday afternoon or under floodlights, preferably for a European game or a domestic Cup replay, was to be part of something way, way out of the ordinary. The excitement generated by the heaving mass with banners aloft, shouting, scream-ing and singing – sometimes they seemed to be doing all three at once – affected everybody.

When the time came for Taylor's advice to be fol-lowed, and the seats had to be put in, Merseyside was split. Many saw that Taylor's way was the only way, if the club were to return and make further progress in the European competitions from which they had been barred. Others, myself among them, wanted the Kop to stay as it was, because it had been the spiritual home of many who died in Sheffield and in Brussels before them, possibly even of some who had died in Natal, much further back in time. We felt the Kop should have been preserved. If, when all the rebuilding work around the country had been completed, Anfield had been left as the sole major stadium with an all-standing section, that could have become the most fitting memorial of all. There is rarely trouble on the

Kop, or in any other part of the Anfield Ground. God knows Liverpool as a city has its share of mindless morons, and worse, but the Kop is sacred. 'Honest John' McKenna had said, when re-opening the roofed-over Kop sixty years earlier: 'We cannot live in the past, but the past should be an inspiration for the present.' Unfortunately, those who ruled, at Anfield and in the wider football world outside, took no heed of McKenna. They felt that Taylor could not be resisted, not even in one small part of the soccer globe. The terracing where so many had stood and swayed, sung and screamed, was ripped out, and seats went in.

Capacity is now around 12,000, approximately half what it used to be. It's a comfortable spot for fans to watch from, much more comfortable than in the old days, but the atmosphere is not the same. Only on really special occasions – against Everton and Manchester United, say, or the Blackburn match that ended the 1994/5 season – do the spectators generate that old thunderous backing. On the playing side, something went out of Liverpool when they lost to Wimbledon at Wembley in 1988, and something else went when they failed to keep hold of the Championship in the following year, losing to Arsenal after having one hand and all but the thumb of the other around the trophy's handles. On the more obvious side, something drained out of Anfield after Heysel, and something else went after Hillsborough. The spirit of helpfulness, the sense of mass comradeship, the sheer delight of being part of something special: all these declined in intensity. Add the growth of anti-social behaviour and the increased use of foul language that are symptoms of modern life wherever you go in this green and pleasant land, and an afternoon or evening on the Kop is now little different from an afternoon or evening at any major football ground.

Things used to be so different. The Kop has played a huge role in the history of Liverpool, club and city, and I have my own special memories, even before the singing, chanting and banner-waving became folklore. When I started watching Liverpool, at the end of World War Two, there were only cheers and the occasional jeer, usually aimed at players lacking determination in the tackle. The encouragement given to the team was just about as constant as constant could be, even in bad times. In the last match of 1952/3, for instance, Liverpool had to beat Chelsea to be absolutely sure of avoiding relegation. The noise when Bill Jones scored the first goal was incredible: when the big, awkward Louis Bimpson added a second near the end, the racket became louder. You could hardly believe that 40,000 or so people could make such a din. In the following season, Bimpson scored three against Manchester United and four, all in the first half, against Burnley to achieve hero status, even though relegation duly arrived a few months later. Bimpson's case proved that you did not have to be a world-class player to become a Kop favourite (though it helps) and that once you have the Koppites behind you, roaring out their support for your every move, you can – sometimes – achieve things you never knew you could. Opponents, too, frequently gained tributes from the generally fair-minded fans on that enormous banking. Late on in that relegation season, Cardiff lost their goalkeeper through injury and full-back Alf Sherwood took over. He helped his team win 1–0, even saving a penalty from Billy Liddell, who was pretty much a certainty when the ball was on the spot. You should have heard the roar of praise . . . and Sherwood was pushing Liverpool into Division Two!

'Real' goalkeepers such as Peter Shilton and Gordon Banks were given ovations every time they turned out at Anfield, although Shilton also felt the sharp edge of Kop humour when, on his first appearance after a well-publicised marital indiscretion, he was greeted with choruses of *Who Were You With Last Night?* Banks had his career ended when he lost an eye in a car crash after playing at Liverpool, for Stoke, on the previous day. 'I didn't intend my last match to be in front of the Kop,' he said. 'But there's nowhere better for a player to finish.' There was another remarkable tribute to the Koppites after a tremendous match in April 1969, when Leeds drew 0–0 and took the point they needed to make certain of the First Division title. Liverpool had had to win to stand any chance of catching up (eventually they finished second with sixty-one points, equalling the record for the highest total ever achieved by a club failing to top that particular table). At the finish Leeds, widely disliked anywhere outside Yorkshire, went to the Kop and were greeted by a tremendous ovation, almost as if Liverpool were the champions. Next day a telegram arrived from Don Revie, the Leeds manager, addressed to 'The Kop,

Anfield, Liverpool' and saying 'Thanks for your very warmhearted gesture. We nominate you as the sportsmen of the century.' Somehow, I cannot visualise the same happening these days, neither the ovation nor the reaction to it. Big-time football has become such a business that it is now conducted in rather too poisonous an atmosphere, no matter how thrilling some of the games might be. This also applies to Anfield, where the Kop humour has been replaced, to a considerable extent, by the moronic chanting of obscenities aimed at opponents, especially black ones. And at the police. No longer is there such a matey, jokey rapport between those who are there to keep the peace and those who sometimes are inclined to disrupt it.

As in society as a whole, people who go to Anfield tend to have lost respect for and trust in the police, who in return are sometimes disinclined to show the tolerance that distinguished the previous guardians, such as Sergeant James 'Walrus' Hesketh, an enormous personality of the 1950s. Hesketh, florid face, giant moustache and all, kept order among far bigger numbers of fans with far smaller numbers of officers on duty than you would find today. Once, struggling past a queue outside the Kop on my way to the press box (lucky, eh?), I saw a man with a burning cigarette between his lips and his arms pressed to his sides by the mass of people. His nose was in danger of being set alight until a mounted bobby, seemingly yards high in the sky, bent from the saddle, took the dog-end from the man's lips, and crushed it between gloved finger and gloved thumb. 'Let dat be a lesson,' he said to the fan. 'Ciggies are no good to yer. Dey make yer ribs 'urt.'

The police did (still do) a good job, especially on the frequent days when the Kop was bursting with heaving bodies outside individual control, being carried yards downwards and back again, or from side to side, as people craned and stretched to follow the action in front of them. At the final whistle, many a fan was lifted up and off the steps and down the other side with his feet dangling above the ground. The sight of people being passed overhead, hand to hand, after fainting or becoming otherwise distressed, was quite common in the early post-war years of boom attendances and few counter-attractions. There was overcrowding elsewhere, and earlier, too. I recall a colleague on the *Echo*, Harold Wolfe, telling me of a Cup tie with Tranmere in 1934 when people scrambled into the stands to escape the crush in the paddock. I remembered that in later years. Koppites might well have been involved in a disaster on their own patch long before they were involved at Brussels and Sheffield. Being an ambulanceman at Anfield in those days was a notably arduous task, and probably still is. Amazingly, serious injuries at the ground have been very rare, although there have been two deaths from heart failure to my knowledge, and one birth (mum, thankfully, had been lifted out of the mass and taken to a safer place before the delivery). Nowadays a computer system keeps track of spectator numbers everywhere in the ground – much more easily done with fans seated rather than standing – and there is little possibility of any overcrowding. That at least is one benefit of the modern age. Forty years ago the system was nowhere near as sophisticated.

My father had been present at Bolton in 1946, when thirty-three people were killed and some 400 injured after crush barriers collapsed at a Cup tie, and he sometimes used his column in the *Liverpool Echo*, 'Ranger's Notes on Sport', to point out the dangers of allowing too many people into one part of the ground, because even the Kop's huge capacity was sometimes insufficient and the exterior stairs were a potential for disaster because of the numbers using them at the same time. Not much happened apart from the board becoming upset (I recall one particularly fierce row Dad had with one of the directors, George Richards, on this subject) and there must have been several narrow escapes. In the end, sadly, Ranger was shown to be right, though not at Anfield: in 1971 sixty-six people died at Ibrox Park, suffocated on stairway 13.

Before then there had been some hairy nights at Anfield in the early European years, notably against Celtic and then against Ajax, when the fans were soaked, the ground was jammed full, and steam rose like smoke from the heaving bodies. When Celtic had a goal disallowed I feared a riot, with bottles raining down despite the advice from the opposite end: the Kop, of course, chanting 'Behave yourself, behave yourself'. On both nights people had difficulty following the game because of the distraction of the seemingly endless lines of stretcher cases being taken away.

Again, a possible tragedy was averted when a snow-storm caused the postponement of a game against Cologne, with a full house in and mostly unable to get out, because the turnstiles could revolve only one way. As the snow continued to fall, the Koppites – and others – invaded the pitch and had an impromptu game with an old busted ball. They had snowball fights, built snowmen, tried to skate, all in good humour. But it could have been very nasty. This was in pre-shoot-out days, and the tie lasted six weeks, from a 0–0 draw in Germany to a toss-up at a play-off in Rotterdam, drawn 2–2 after extra time. In between there had been the no-match snow match and another 0–0 draw. Like many Brits who have memories of the war years, I suppose, I have no particular affinity with Germany and Germans, but the Cologne team earned a lot of sympathy. The sight of Yeats and others leaping for joy as the referee's red and white disc came down red side up (after sticking on its edge first time) remains unforgettable, but no team deserves to lose after play-ing three matches, five hours in all, without being beaten.

There had been the usual faithful Red followers in Cologne and in Rotterdam, as there always were and still are and presumably always will be. For the big occasions, and there have been plenty of those, the Kop virtually grows wheels and travels to the destination, no matter how far. Wembley often has been awash with red, the community singing sabotaged, the opposing fans shouted down. Foreign cities have trembled before the invasion and there has been trouble; of course there has, in volatile situations with unlimited access to strange and potent types of beverage. In general, though, the huge majority of Liverpool fans have been pretty well behaved on their travels. (All the more sad, therefore, that their reputation should be so fearfully and unforgivably besmirched at Heysel.) The greatest day of all was in Rome on the occasion of the club's first appearance in a Champions Cup final. Estimates vary, but there were many, many thousands of Red fans in the 57,000 crowd, far too many of them having had to endure awful journeys by train and coach across Europe. The place seemed full of Scousers, the forest of banners and flags growing larger as the game went on. Before and after, the Koppites took over much of the city centre in a powerful but almost totally peaceful celebration, marvellous to behold. The route to the Olympic Stadium was lined with stalls selling all kinds of souvenirs. At one, a blind guitarist sang and played, while his son rattled the tin. Behind him, the wall carried the message 'Cesare Ferrari welcomes you' in various languages. Only the English version was different: a Koppite (it must have been a Koppite) had slipped past the singer and the son, crossed out the name and substituted 'Gordon Lee' – much criticised manager of a then not-too-powerful Everton. Cruel, yes, but a typical example of Kop humour.

For years after that amazing night in Rome, the pop tunes continued to be belted forth, the thousands swayed and swung, laps of honour were the end-of-season norm, and all seemed well with the Kop's world. And so it continued, until Heysel and Hillsborough.

In between those two catastrophes, there had been another lucky escape for the Kop and those who stood there. A check on the safety barriers in 1987 revealed that some of them needed replacing, having been weakened over the years. Further investigations revealed that a large wastepipe connected to the main sewer running under the Kop was in danger of collapse, after being in place for about eighty years. That in turn could have caused the main sewer to break up, which might have led to a collapse of part of the terracing. If that had happened during a match, the outcome does not bear thinking about. As it was, the first three scheduled home matches that season had to be postponed, and Koppites and the other fans had to wait for their first view of the new heroes, Beardsley and Barnes, appearing on their own pitch.

So the Kop, revered as it was, had been lucky to avoid mass injury to its inhabitants down the years, and eventually the time came for the seats to be installed, mostly in red with the huge letters 'LFC' picked out in white. There are now much easier entrance and exit routes, better toilet facilities (meaning an end to the old cry of 'Roll up yer *Echo*' when access to the old loos was spectator-jammed impossible) and the view is clear at all times. On the last day of the standing Kop's existence, 30 April 1994, some of the old heroes appeared for another cheer – Liddell, Stubbins, Callaghan, Tommy Smith, Dalglish and Phil Thompson among them. And then the team went and lost to Norwich City. Jeremy Goss got the only goal, and a good one it was too, but Liverpool's failure to equalise meant that the last Liverpool player to score in front of the old Kop was the one I have admired least out of all the hundreds I have seen: Julian Dicks, who had scored in the previous home game, against Ipswich, from a penalty. The fact that a player as undisciplined as Dicks could become a hero during his short spell at Anfield indicated, to me at least, that the modern Kop has different values from the old Kop.

Five years to the day before Dicks scored that goal, people had been arriving in their thousands to pay tribute to those who died at Hillsborough. The Kop first, then the pitch, then other parts of the ground, gradually disappeared under the mounds of flowers, scarves, shirts and other items laid by the grieving living, in memory of the cruelly snatched dead. The response to the disaster was amazing, even in a city that, for all its apparent toughness, often sheds collective tears. Some people travelled thousands of miles to be there. I know of one fan who went there from Norway, and back, in a day; former player Craig Johnston, who had taken some stick from the Kop in his time, made the trip from Australia. I watched TV and wept, and was unable to force myself to go. Now I very much regret that failure to do so. The early summer sun shone, and the crowds moved slowly in silence. *You'll Never Walk Alone*, the anthem of all soccer anthems, was stilled. The flowers piled up and football was forgotten. Those were incomparable days: the greatest days of the Kop's life.

Chapter Three

Shanks, man of the people

The scene: Prenton Park, Tranmere, on a late summer evening in the mid-1950s. Workington had just forced a 1–1 draw and their manager was talking to the few journalists present. I can see him now, wearing a neat suit and a raincoat, hands in the pockets of his trousers, and I can hear him now, Scottish burr buzzing away. 'My goalkeeper, Wilf Billington, will be in the English team within a few years,' he said. Wilf who? You have to have a deep knowledge of players of that time to recall Billington, who had a couple of seasons with Workington, then sank without trace. In soccer terms he was never within 1,000 miles of a call to the England colours. But I bet he often felt that he was a better goalkeeper than his mediocre record indicates, simply because his manager told him so.

That was my first meeting with Bill Shankly, eternal optimist in all things, but a football man first and last. You do not readily forget your first meeting with a legend, even if he was not a legend at the time. Something about Shankly's manner that evening, when he was the none-too-successful manager of a none-too-successful club, stuck in my mind. When, a few years later, he pitched up at Anfield (having earlier turned down an offer because he had been told that the directors would carry on picking the team), I believed him when he said that he would turn the club round. He had been waiting for a big club to give him a chance. He was given a salary of £2,000 a year, sole charge of the playing staff, and the promise that money would be made available for new players.

For a man who used so many brief sentences, Shankly was surprisingly fond of the odd flowery phrase. One, which he often repeated, was that 'Liverpool FC were a footballing giant who had been dormant far too long'. Shankly poked that giant in the ribs and disturbed its slumbers, slowly at first, until it suddenly burst into life with a roar that is still reverberating around the football world over thirty years later. There is no doubt that Shankly did an enormous amount for the city of Liverpool, for the club, the players and the supporters who took him to their hearts because they realised, from the start, that he was one of their own. After one of the three League Championships won during his time at Anfield, Shankly accompanied the team on their lap of honour, and trod on a red and white scarf lying on the cinder track in front of the Kop. He picked it up and put it round his neck, saying: 'We can't leave that scarf in the dirt. That's somebody's life.' After the 1974 FA Cup final win against Newcastle, two fans got on to the pitch, lay in front of Shankly, and kissed his shoes. 'Give them a polish while you're down there, lads,' he said. A faintly embarrassing incident, but one indicative of the regard in which he was held by ordinary supporters.

The Shankly rebuilding of the Anfield edifice coincided with the growth of pop culture and, with not inconsiderable help from Everton, established the city in the public eye, not merely in England but in many other countries. Although some of his statements were outrageous ('I can't understand Ajax, playing defensively on their own ground' after Liverpool had lost 1–5) and some of his forecasts were wildly over-optimistic, he became a major figure in football who loved being popular but never allowed that popularity to corrupt his basic nature. His unexpected retirement in July 1974 caused widespread dismay, but Liverpool went on to even greater things without him. By the time of his death in September 1981, aged sixty-seven, there was little doubt that the love affair between the little Scot and his former employers had soured somewhat, but the fans still adored him.

And how good a manager was he? Perhaps not as good as many people think: the glow still shines, after two decades, but distance could be lending an extra sheen to the light that blinded so many during the days when Shankly strode the Anfield stage like James Cagney, one of the stars of the gangster movies he loved so dearly. In *White Heat*, Cagney, playing a mother-fixated hoodlum, screams, 'Look at me now, ma – top of the world,' from the highest point on a gasometer; Shankly's admiration for the actor may have blinded him to the fact that a few seconds later Cagney's character was spectacularly dead, blown up by the explosion he had caused.

Shankly revelled in the role of a small man become big, and he had every reason to be proud. As a player, he earned a reputation as one of the best wing-halves of the 1930s, having worked his way from an Ayrshire colliery village to Carlisle and then, after only sixteen senior games, to Preston. 'There were only two things in Scotland in those days,' he would say. 'The pit, and football. Football was better.' As one of ten children (one of his brothers, Robert, preceded him as a manager, with Dundee United), the young William soon learned the value of money. He grew up a teetotal non-smoker, perhaps as much for financial reasons as for his health because in later years he liked a good party (as so many non-drinkers do) as much as he liked a good argument, and one was an inevitable lead-in to the other. He could be brash before an audience, and often was, but he had considerable charm and, although far from a Casanova, he often fascinated female company (my step-mother, for one). He would boast that during his playing days, which covered fifteen 'proper' seasons plus the war years, he was never left out of the Preston team until his last few weeks. Injury and the odd call to Scotland's colours – he won five full caps – were the rare and only reasons why he lost his place. When the time came to answer the call he reputedly handed his number four jersey to the young man deputed to take over, and said: 'You don't have to do anything with that, son. It runs round by itself.' The youngster, incidentally, was one Tommy Docherty.

Shankly had played in the 1937 FA Cup final, which Preston lost after leading at half-time. Sunderland scored three times in the second half, although Shankly and thousands of fans believed that before they did so a second Preston goal, ruled out for a foul, had been legitimate and would have put North End out of reach. A year later North End returned to Wembley and won by a last-minute penalty, after extra time, against Huddersfield. George Mutch was injured in the incident that led to the award and, as deputy penalty taker, for a moment Shankly thought that the job would be his, but Mutch recovered and scored, off the bar. That win was some consolation for what Shankly described as the biggest disappointment of his career: a few days earlier Preston had lost a vital late-season League game to Arsenal, who went on to win the Championship, and had finished third. Jimmy Milne, the other Preston wing-half that day, was injured early in the game and, with no substitutes in that unenlightened era, Preston lost 3–1. Milne missed the Cup final. By grisly coincidence his son Gordon also missed a Wembley final through injury, in 1965 when he was with Liverpool and Shankly was his manager. By another coincidence, Shankly once missed a penalty while playing for Preston at Anfield – Easter Monday, 1947 – when Liverpool came from nowhere to win the Championship.

Not long after that, Shankly gave up playing and moved into management, having had an offer from his old club Carlisle to succeed player-manager Ivor

Broadis, who had negotiated his own transfer to Sunderland. Shankly had been given a free transfer by Preston but was still very fit at thirty-five. He decided, however, to concentrate solely on the managerial side, although he came to regret the decision because he discovered that no matter how successful a manager becomes, that job is still second to being a player, particularly when you are a player who runs and passes and tackles and cajoles and shouts like Shankly used to do. He had some difficulty persuading the Carlisle board to accept one of his basic theories about football: too many clubs train their men to be marathon runners rather than football players. But he got his way and introduced more ball play and less lapping. In two seasons under his leadership, Carlisle finished ninth and third in the old Third Division (North), and held Arsenal to a goalless draw in a celebrated FA Cup game at Highbury. Arsenal's last Cup tie had been a 2–0 win over Liverpool at Wembley seven months earlier, but this time the Gunners were lucky to escape defeat. 'I'd often played against Reg Lewis,' said Shankly. 'I knew him as a good player and a genuine man. At the end of the game he came up to me and apologised, saying we should have won. We should, too.' Thousands turned out to welcome the team home but when the replay arrived the inspiration had passed even though Carlisle had home advantage, and Arsenal won 4–1 (Lewis scoring twice).

Shankly did not stay much longer at Brunton Park. Grimsby wanted him and he fancied the challenge, taking them very close to promotion in his first full season. They finished second to their closest rivals, Lincoln City. A year later they were fifth, and less than a year after that Shankly moved again. Grimsby were then on their way to a final place in the table of seventeen, and Shankly had been unable to arrest the decline. There was little or no money for him to find the new men he wanted – 'Players who will battle when there is nothing at stake' – and those he had were unresponsive to his demands. He wanted out and his solution was to join people even more desperate than he was. Back to Cumbria, but turning left before Carlisle and carrying on to the outpost of Workington, struggling to stay above water in an isolated area where what few fans there were tended to watch the rugby league team, three times Wembley finalists in the 1950s.

The football club had been elected to the League in 1951 (replacing my first love, New Brighton). In their first season they were bottom. In their second season they were next to bottom. A third successive application for re-election almost certainly would have been doomed to failure. Shankly arrived knowing that if the club's hard-working core of enthusiasts were to keep League soccer alive in the town, he had to do something out of the ordinary. 'When I got there, I felt like I had been to the moon,' he said. 'The journey was awful. No motorways in those days, and the trip took for ever. You could persuade players to talk about moving there, but once they realised how much mileage they would clock up, they lost interest. People could spend years of their lives just going to and from the place.' Despite the problems, Shankly liked

Workington. There he was, the big fish in the smallest football pond he had ever sampled since he left Glenbuck. A few signings paid off – one, Ernie Whittle from Lincoln, kept the club out of the last four almost single-handed with some vital goals – and the gates showed a small but welcome rise. Shanks set about becoming a cult figure with generosity to match his humour and enthusiasm. He once fined a player £20, more than a week's wages, for going 'on the toot' one night, then went to his house a few days later, took him to a shop and bought him a suit, for rather more than that. He gave another player £25 as a wedding present, even though he could not attend for his piece of the cake. As he did at other clubs, he found a player who lived close to a recreation ground and would get him out of bed on a Sunday so that they could join the kids playing.

Then, less than two years after going to Borough Park – having to share the ground with the rugby league team was one problem, having to take a wage cut to help keep the club solvent was another – Shankly became assistant to Andy Beattie, who was managing Huddersfield after a brief spell in charge of Scotland (he had achieved an odd 'distinction' by resigning at the 1954 World Cup in Switzerland; not before it or after it, but while it was on). Shankly and Beattie had played together for Preston and Scotland with considerable success, but that had been several years earlier. Now the alliance was something of a disaster and within a few months Town were relegated from the First Division. Beattie decided to quit and Shankly stayed . . . to be promoted to his old pal's place. Beattie, who had been instrumental in the choice of his assistant, could not have been too happy. Later, in one of the frequent managerial swings-and-roundabouts situations, Beattie became manager of Shankly's old club, Carlisle. Later still, time having done its usual healing job, Shankly took Beattie on to Liverpool's scouting staff.

Shankly was by this time forty-three and had been in management for almost eight years, with little to show for it. Perhaps if he had stayed longer at any one place he might have done better, but then few managers stay rooted for long. More money for the transfer market might have helped, yet Shankly was not alone in being strapped for cash: few managers in lower divisions have much to spare. In the truncated newspapers of the time, with football magazines virtually non-existent and TV and radio rarely let loose on the game, the man later to be a media dream had achieved little more than minor cult status in three small, far-flung spots on the football map. Compared with Carlisle, Grimsby and Workington, however, Huddersfield of the mid-1950s was Ford Consul to Ford Popular. At last Shankly was at a club with tradition (three successive Championships, one FA Cup, lots of near misses) and a proven reputation for finding fresh talent. Yet even here, although he talked a good game and had many fine theories, Shankly was hardly a roaring success. The team were placed twelfth, ninth and fourteenth in the old Division Two in his three full seasons at Leeds Road, and after reaching the fifth round of the Cup in the first of them, they then lost twice in round three.

This despite the presence of some notable players, including Ray Wilson, who was to become one of England's 1966 World Cup winners, Ray Wood (formerly of Manchester United), Len Quested, Bill McGarry and Dave Hickson, an argumentative centre-forward who began at Everton, went to Villa, then to Huddersfield, and was sold by Shankly back to Everton before joining Liverpool just before Shanks arrived. And, of course, there was a skinny Scottish kid by the name of Denis Law, who made his first team debut at sixteen and became renowned as one of Britain's finest players.

The most remarkable event of Shankly's time in charge at Huddersfield happened in December 1957 when Town contrived to lose 7–6 at Charlton after leading 5–1 with twenty minutes to play against a team reduced to ten men. No club before or since has scored six in a League match and lost: was this, I wonder, the day that convinced Shankly of the need for pragmatism instead of romanticism, putting rather more emphasis on defence than on attack? The following year Huddersfield were in turn reduced to ten men in a game but won it 5–0 . . . against Liverpool. In retrospect (always a good place from which to look at things) Liverpool's choice of Shankly to replace Phil Taylor was a decision made in heaven. Yet judging by his record before he arrived at Anfield, he was perhaps a surprising choice. After all, what had he won?

His arrival was due largely to the efforts of one man, T V Williams, then chairman of the Liverpool directors, who was later elected to be the club's first president in recognition of his services. Williams was a man of great warmth and dignity, though inclined to be short-tempered. Something about Shankly had impressed him when their paths had crossed, and he decided that Shanks was the man Liverpool needed. He persuaded the rest of the board that this was the right choice to make if the club were to end their cycle of non-success: since relegation to the Second Division in 1954 they had finished eleventh, third, third, fourth and fourth, and their FA Cup defeats included one by Southend and another by non-League Worcester City. Shankly's last match in charge of Huddersfield was a 1–0 win over Liverpool, and his first in charge of Liverpool, on 19 December 1959, was a 0–4 home defeat by Cardiff, a margin that has been repeated at Anfield only once in the thirty-five years since. That was the last occasion on which a Liverpool board chose the team, Shankly having declined to do so because he had not then had the chance to see all the players in action. He made only two changes for the next game, a 0–3 reverse at Charlton, but after that he presided over a run of six wins and two draws, interrupted only by a 1–3 home Cup knockout by Manchester United on a day when the crowd, for once, rarely raised any sort of racket. Third, again, was the final League placing and only four of the eleven home League games between Shankly's arrival and the season's end attracted crowds above 30,000.

Clearly there was a lot to do, and gradually the new man set about the necessary rebuilding of the club's image as well as of the playing staff. The great Billy

Liddell at last closed his career (he played only twelve games under Shankly) and the teenager Ian Callaghan was among those tried. Gordon Milne (who went on to get fourteen England caps) became Shankly's first signing and several old faces disappeared. But third, once more, was not good enough. Nor was an average attendance of 29,603, Liverpool's lowest post-war average. At that stage, T V Williams might have been having a doubt or two.

The first of the two major signings that were to transform Liverpool happened just as the 1960/1 season ended. Shankly had kept faith with Hickson, and so had the crowd, who had overlooked his Everton history and treated him more kindly than anyone might have expected. But he was over thirty, had been bat-tered by many a defender, and was no longer the right partner for Hunt, who had scored thirty-six goals in his first sixty-eight games. Shankly went for Ian St John of Motherwell, and signed him for £37,500. St John had time for one game, a Liverpool Senior Cup match at Goodison Park, before summer stopped play. He scored a hat-trick and became part of the local folklore, just as he had done at Motherwell, where he was reputed to have scored three times in under three minutes during one game. He was followed by Ron Yeats, a big man in every way, signed for £30,000 from Dundee United after first causing Shankly to blink by asking: 'Where's Liverpool?' The fees seem ridiculously tiny in comparison with today's figures, but appeared huge at the time and caused some anguish among a board of directors not renowned for heavy spending.

Their fears were soon put to rest, though, for both St John and Yeats earned a Second Division Championship medal in the first of their several seasons at Anfield after opening with ten wins and a draw in their first eleven games. 'I thought they would make a difference,' said Shankly. 'I didn't expect them to make such a big one.'

By now Anfield gates were up, the Shankly aura was spreading and locally based journalists could no longer supplement their incomes by reporting Liverpool games for the bigger papers: the bigger papers were now sending their own writers to matches regularly, as a preliminary to basing their own full-time staff on Merseyside. There was plenty for them to write about, for Liverpool resumed life in the First Division by showing that they were capable of repeating their form from the Second. With Willie Stevenson from Rangers adding class in midfield they reached the FA Cup semi-final, losing to a Leicester team inspired by goalkeeper Gordon Banks. They finished only eighth in the table but for a time had title hopes, until a 7–2 crash at Tottenham on Easter Monday was followed by only one win in the last eight games. More than thirty years later, Jimmy Greaves of Spurs remained the last man to put four goals into a Liverpool net in one match. Two changes for the following season set Liverpool on the title path again. Alf Arrowsmith settled in alongside Hunt up front, with St John dropping back in place of Melia, and Peter Thompson came from Preston to play on the left flank. A strong combination of non-stop effort and fluent passing, plus a great deal of individual skill, took the Reds to an uncatchable position with three games still to play – after the first three home matches had been lost. 'Gentlemen,' Shankly told a packed room after the third, 'I assure you that we *will* win a home match this season.' By that time he was in a position where he could joke about a situation that might have had other managers tensing their back muscles in anticipation of the dagger.

That position was strengthened beyond any possible onslaught in 1964/5, when Liverpool at last won the FA Cup for the first time, and reached the European Cup semi-final. They were reinforced by two local products, Smith and Lawler, with Strong from Arsenal as the only new import. Poor Arrowsmith disappeared from view after damaging cruciate ligaments in the season-opening Charity Shield, but even so there were six 'homegrown' products in the Wembley team all of whom had been at Anfield since before Shankly's arrival, compared with five buys, all having proved to be bargains. 'The right blend – that's what matters,' said Shanks, and in 1965/6 Liverpool won the Championship again and reached the Cup Winners' Cup final, but their most remarkable feat was that of going through the entire season of fifty-two matches using only fifteen players, Arrowsmith making only four appearances, Graham one and Chisnall one. Hercules, whoever he played for, could not have laboured harder than the twelve regulars. This was a wonderful performance of sustained skill and consistency, but I was not alone in feeling that the load was too great. Substitutes were now allowed yet Liverpool used their twelfth man in only three of those fifty-two fixtures, even when several games were clearly won with time to spare and players such as Hunt, Thompson and Byrne, all of whom were in the England World Cup squad, could have done with a breather. Shankly was not alone; British managers in general were slow to catch on to the benefits of the new rule. (Now, of course, the facility is being done to death.) Shankly, who had rejoiced in his own fitness when running the Preston midfield, tended to treat injured players as somehow suspect, and he carried that to extremes, as on the occasion when one man, complaining of having 'done something to my leg', was allegedly told: 'That's not your leg, it's Liverpool's leg.' A true story? Maybe not, but it sounds quite likely. Shankly's justification was that the adrenalin of the dual League and Europe chase kept players at their peak. But the Liverpool team that lost to Borussia Dortmund in the final certainly looked terribly jaded, despite the joy of having clinched the domestic title a few days earlier.

This was the start of a period of comparative decline in which Shankly's personal increase in stature was not matched by his team's performances. After a title in each of three seasons, not a single one was won in the next six (Liverpool finished fifth, third, second, fifth, fifth and third), with little distinction in Europe and the FA Cup, and the same applying to the League Cup to which entry was now compulsory. There was still a great deal of excellent football played, with many magnificent matches and big gates, but – even if those with short memories find it hard to believe – Liverpool lost their place as the top English club to the likes of Leeds and Arsenal. Shankly perhaps kept his trust in the 1962 to 1966 nucleus for too long. Emlyn Hughes from Blackpool was the only signing of 1967, too late to make much difference that season, and Tony Hateley from Chelsea was the only addition the following year. Hateley, who cost £96,000, had a reasonably successful season but left for Coventry after four games in 1968/9, bringing in only £80,000. This was an example of Shankly's occasionally impulsive methods in the market. Hateley was promptly replaced by Alun Evans, British football's first £100,000 teenager, who had a remarkable start. He scored the third of Liverpool's four goals in the first twelve minutes against Leicester (it finished only 4–0) and a week later he scored twice in a 6–0 win away to his former club, Wolves. When a 4–0 result at Burnley a week later completed a Liverpool run of five successive victories, with eighteen goals scored and none conceded, Shankly, not surprisingly, was elated. 'There is nothing that can stop Alun Evans from playing for England,' he said. True, Evans had looked the part, briefly, but time soon showed that Shankly was suffering from overenthusiasm. As with Workington's Wilf Billington all those years before, his confidence was misplaced. True, Evans was unlucky, never the same after his face had been badly damaged in a nightclub scrap. But he was not big enough or strong enough to be a top striker, and a couple of years later Shankly was glad to get £65,000 for him, from Aston Villa, after he had scored only thirty-three goals in 110 games.

One of Evans's last appearances was in the 1971 FA Cup final defeat by Arsenal, when, after an excellent display against Everton in the semi-final, he hardly put a foot right and was substituted in the second half. By now Liverpool had several new faces, with Heighway breaking through from amateur football, Toshack having arrived from Cardiff, and Lloyd and Lindsay in a defence which now had Clemence in goal for Lawrence, scapegoat for a surprise FA Cup defeat at Watford the previous season. The excitement of the boiling hot day at Wembley, when Arsenal came from one down in extra time to win, disguised the fact that this was a dull season for Liverpool whose forty-two League games had generated a record low total of sixty-six goals (forty-two for and twenty-four against). Around this time it was hard to resist the conclusion that Shankly's safety-first policy, built up over several seasons of European competition, was being carried too far, and that Liverpool were sometimes too ready to settle for a draw instead of chasing a win. Their preoccupation with defence certainly cost them dearly in the 1971 Fairs Cup semi-final when they lost at home to a Bremner goal in the first leg, and again were unable to break through the Leeds defence in the second.

This cautious outlook changed somewhat the following season when Keegan and Cormack arrived. Keegan's remarkable rise, from being perched on a dustbin for photographers on the day he signed to becoming perhaps the first of soccer's modern millionaires, has been well documented. Nobody knew that he would do as well as he did, but he got the breaks early in his debut against Forest, in the first game of the season, and never looked back. Cormack, too, had a splendid start without winning the superlatives that Shankly lavished on KK, although he disappeared pretty quickly after falling out of favour three years later, by which time he and Keegan had helped Liverpool to the Championship and Uefa Cup Double in 1972/3, and to the FA Cup in the following season. By then everyone had forgotten about the failure of two comparatively expensive strikers, Jack Whitham (sixteen games, seven goals) and Alan Waddle (sixteen games, one goal – against Everton). Not all Shankly buys were bargains, though most of them were.

Not long after the demolition of Newcastle at Wembley, Little Big Man retired. I will never forget the moment, hearing the news on the car radio as I was driving along a narrow residential street, and just avoiding a parked van as I momentarily lost my grip on the wheel. A well remembered vox pop TV interview on the city streets revealed fan after disbelieving fan stunned by the news. 'Yer 'avin' us on' was the general tenor of the answers. 'Shankly's retired?' queried one fan. 'Has the Pope retired as well?' Later, the reports of the media conference struck some rather strange chords. Shankly spoke of needing a rest and recharging his batteries, even – Cagneyesque to the last – of going to see the chairman 'feeling like I was going to the electric chair'. Why, then, did he go to the training ground a couple of hours later to complete the signing of one of the club's best captures of all, Ray Kennedy? The chairman, John (later Sir John) Smith, said that the board had accepted Shankly's decision with extreme reluctance, and thanked him for the magnificent job he had done, but there was no mention of any effort to dissuade the man from going. Nor was there an announcement that Bob Paisley would take over; that best known of all secrets was not confirmed until more than a week later. Something, somewhere, seemed not quite right about it all.

Shankly left a strong team and a strong club, rebuilt to a large extent during his time in charge. He was particularly fond of the improvements, which he had instigated, to the training ground at Melwood. Success had brought Liverpool undreamt of wealth. Not long afterwards Shanks received the OBE for his services to soccer, followed by a testimonial that drew 40,000 fans. He seemed set for a long and happy retirement, shared with his wife and his dog in their house near the Everton training ground at Bellefield. (Legend claims he bought that particular house so he could walk the dog, with all that activity entails, on Everton property, and that the first job he did on moving in was to paint the bathroom red and white.) He admitted that in nearly fifteen years in Liverpool he had taken his wife out on non-football business twice, although he denied the tale that he took Nessie to see Rochdale reserves as an anniversary treat. 'Not true,' he said. 'Would I get married in the football season?' But the retirement was none too long and, I fear, none too happy. After a while Shankly would have welcomed a chance to go back to Anfield in some official capacity, but he was not given that chance. He turned up at

Melwood regularly for a while, then the visits became less frequent. Although Melwood and the routines there had Shankly's stamp, time passed and several of the faces changed. Where the faces stayed the same, perhaps the attitudes changed instead. I have clear evidence of one particular great event in the club's post-Shankly history at which the reaction of others when he tried to become involved proved how clearly, and how sadly, he had become yesterday's man.

Shankly had realised quite soon in his retirement that he was lost without a job in football. I believe he even tried to get back on the staff, causing a certain understandable friction with the board and with Paisley, his old friend and colleague, now his successor and doing very nicely, thank you. And when an unfortunate autobiography appeared it did nothing to narrow the gap that had developed. He spent more time with his two married daughters. He dabbled a bit at Tranmere, where Yeats was then manager. He had a radio phone-in programme for a time, and appeared on *This Is Your Life*. And all the time football went on, and he was very much out of it. To the public, however, Shanks remained an idol, and there was widespread grief and many genuine tributes when he died, seven years after leaving the club. I remembered that grim touch of humour he had showed when he said that after his death he would like people to file past his coffin and say: 'Aye, there lies a fit man.' But not even a man as fit as Shankly could withstand two heart attacks in seventy-two hours. The city's flags flew at half-mast and boats sounded their sirens along the Mersey. At the funeral service they played *You'll Never Walk Alone* and the Shankly Gates at Anfield were erected in commemoration of him. At least he was spared the horrors of Heysel and Hillsborough.

Scotland has a reputation for producing legendary managers from poorish backgrounds. Shankly followed Busby, was contemporary with Stein – 'You're immortal, John,' said Shanks after Celtic had won the European Cup – and preceded Ferguson and Dalglish. Whether he was the best of them all is a question that has no answer. He eventually touched great heights, after a moderate start as a manager, even though he won 'only' seven major trophies – the Second Division, the Championship three times, FA Cup twice and Uefa Cup once – but how many managers win more than one or two? As a coach, he kept the game simple and based the success of his Liverpool teams on fitness, hard work, determination and team spirit, supplemented by the ability to pass accurately and the patience to keep on doing it until opponents were worn down and caught out. Above all, he instilled confidence in his men by that combination of common sense and over-exaggeration that made him unique. When Emlyn Hughes said 'Everything I achieved in football, I owed to Shanks', he was speaking for many others besides himself. If the passing of the seasons has added somewhat to the Shankly legend rather than diminished it, then that is a good and merited thing. He brought enormous pleasure to countless millions on Merseyside and far, far beyond that corner of England. A football man, first and last.

Chapter Four
Uncle Bob, and his followers

Bob Paisley thought his first season as Liverpool manager was a failure. The club were second in the League table, two points behind Derby, went out of Europe after only two ties, lost at home to Middlesbrough – inspired by a certain Graeme Souness – in the fourth round of the League Cup, and lost at Ipswich in the second stage of the FA Cup. 'Ah thought that we simply had to win something otherwise everybody would say Ah wasn't up to the job of following Bill Shankly,' said Paisley. Things were to get rather better after that . . .

Kevin Keegan might have been the man to blame for Paisley's failure to win a trophy in 1974/5. He certainly got the new chief's managerial years off to a bad start when he was sent off, with Billy Bremner of Leeds, at Wembley of all places, in the FA Charity Shield. Four days earlier Keegan had been sent off in a pre-season friendly in Germany and the inevitable suspensions caused him to miss nine matches. The team surely would not have dropped the seven points that they did in those nine games if Keegan had been playing. That particular problem is easily recalled when discussing Paisley's early managerial role. Not many remember that, at the same time, Larry Lloyd was left out of the team at Wembley and for the first League match, made grumbling sounds and, perhaps to his surprise, was a Coventry player within a few days. Paisley, a genial Geordie with an expansive laugh – something Shankly rarely revealed – was going to be his own man.

Paisley had waited a long time to become manager, and when the chance happened he was fifty-five years of age and, ironically, was not sure if he wanted to take it. As a player, he had won the FA Amateur Cup with Bishop Auckland, then joined Liverpool just before World War Two broke out. He was a tough wing-half who played over 200 games in eight seasons, winning a Championship medal in 1947 but being controversially left out of the (losing) FA Cup final team three years later. Ironically the FA Cup was the only trophy his Liverpool teams contested and did not win under his management: in the space of the eight seasons after his 'disaster' first year they won six Championships, three League Cups, three European Cups and one Uefa Cup, plus the Charity Shield five times and the European Super Cup once. In five of those seasons they won two major trophies, and in each of the other three years they won one. It is a record without parallel in English football history, all the more remarkable because it was achieved by a man who took the job reluctantly.

Of course Paisley inherited a good team from Shankly, and a good playing pattern. The two had worked closely for several years, and Paisley had had ample experience as a physiotherapist and trainer, and as assistant before the top job finally became his. But Paisley was not afraid to experiment or to back his own judgment of players. For example, Ray Kennedy, a striker not always pure and certainly not simple when with Arsenal, had been the last Shankly signing. He lacked pace, struggled up front, and seemed set for a brief stay until Paisley switched him to midfield to the advantage of player, club and country. Phil Neal, who had been around Northampton for a while without a big club going for him, became Paisley's first signing, eventually supplanted Lindsay, and turned into a ten-year fixture who won fifty England caps. Terry McDermott, a Scouser, came back to his spiritual home when Paisley prised him from Newcastle's midfield. To be more precise, he came back from his bed one lunch-time, where he was still in repose after a cultural tour of Tyneside nightspots. That sort of scenario would have been too much for Shankly, but Paisley saw the more dedicated side of McDermott. David Johnson, another Liverpudlian not entirely unfamiliar with fleshpots, was signed from Ipswich, and he and Terry Mac both worked hard enough and well enough to wear the England jersey. So did Alan Kennedy, once a clubmate of McDermott's at Newcastle, and Sammy Lee, who defied the twin handicaps of too much weight and too little height to become yet another inter-national.

As for the other nationalities, look at the list and

wonder at Paisley's eye for talent. Irishmen Mark Lawrenson (born in Preston) and Ronnie Whelan. Scotsmen Alan Hansen from Partick, Graeme Souness from Middlesbrough and Steve Nicol from Ayr, all top-rank players who represented their country (in Hansen's case by no means as often as he deserved), plus the incomparable Kenny Dalglish from Celtic. Welshmen Ian Rush and Joey Jones. Rush did not score in his first nine appearances for Liverpool after his move from Chester. 'You're supposed to be a striker – be more selfish,' said Paisley. Lo and behold, one touch of Uncle Bob's magic wand and Rush was on his way to soccer immortality. And then there was Jones, a cult figure if ever there was one, a Koppite incarnate, an aggressive player, tattoos and all, who never looked as good as the list of caps against his name – eventually reaching seventy-two – would make him out to be. Paisley, who had endured a bit of barracking in his playing days, knew the inspirational value of having popular players, the sort who have the crowd on their side even when not doing well. Not many full-backs become as popular as Joey was at Anfield, and although he had only three seasons before being sold back to his first club, Wrexham, he cannot be classed as a failure. Nor can Craig Johnston, although he was wildly inconsistent and quit soccer when only twenty-seven to care for his sick sister, and to become a photographer, a songwriter and an inventor of a new type of football boot. Johnston was a one-off, often in arguments, but he became a true Red. He tra-velled back from Australia to pay his respects at the shrine that Anfield became after Hillsborough, and was at the Kop's closing ceremony as well. Another foreign-born Paisley import, Grobbelaar, gave great value for money and was a splendid entertainer. Indeed, that can be said about nearly all the players who moved to Anfield during Paisley's period in charge. They could play, and they could play in an entertaining way.

Of the Englishmen he signed, only two did not live up to expectations: David Hodgson from Middlesbrough, and Richard Money from Fulham. Kevin MacDonald, a Scot from Leicester, also failed to do himself justice while at Anfield (he had several injury problems), although he played quite a part in the late surge that earned the Double in 1986. Avi Cohen, an Israeli international, did little apart from become a trivia statistic: his twenty-three appearances were spread over four competitions, and he scored his only goal, against Aston Villa, in a Championship-deciding match in 1980, as well as scoring one for Villa. After a period back in Israel he returned to Britain, at the age of thirty, and joined Souness at Rangers. Briefly.

Collectively, Liverpool dropped around £500,000 after the eventual sales of Hodgson, Money, MacDonald and Cohen, a reasonably large sum a decade ago, peanuts now. But if you compare that amount with the benefits brought in by Paisley's better signings, the gap is immeasurable. Nine of the men Paisley bought appear in my all-time Liverpool XI (see chapter 6), and they are there for three main reasons: talent, willingness to learn, and personal courage. These attributes were top of Paisley's list when he went talent-spotting. Skill, obviously, as well but he had no time for men who thought they knew all there was to know about the game, and no time for men who would not battle. Link that to the Shankly creed of keeping it simple and always passing to a red shirt, and the recipe for success was as complete as any club's could hope to be. If Callaghan, Smith, Case, Phil Thompson, Fairclough and Lee were the only really notable local products to appear during his reign, they were not a bad half-dozen to have on call, were they? And while success generated such income, why let the taxman get it? Why not spend it on ready-made products? At least the money stayed in the game, even if the rich clubs cornered a dispro- portionate amount of talent. The art of spending money on players, of course, is to spend it on the right players. Shankly usually did so by scouting in the lower divisions whereas Paisley set his sights on more expens- ive produce. Both carried out this difficult job remark- ably well.

Paisley, I believe, has never been given the credit he deserves for what he did for English football, let alone Liverpool football. Shankly was the personality, the pseudo-Godfather figure, the media man's delight, but Paisley's achievements dwarf even Shankly's excellent record. Not just at club level, but on the wider scene. Paisley did not get the same media attention, perhaps because he was not as fluent a speaker. He could be just as amusing, but a conversation with Paisley was, on occasion, difficult because his speech was full of wotsits and doings and thingumajigs, which he of course understood but others could not always comprehend. It was an endearing trait; unfortunately for the media people it was a trait not made for the electronic age. So Paisley, usually to his delight, often went uninterviewed while he was building, and after he had built, his unique place in the game's history.

Until Uncle Bob took Liverpool back into the European Champions Cup after the virginal forays under Shanks, Britain could not compare with the Spaniards, Italians, Dutch and Germans. All England and Scotland had to show for twenty-one seasons of effort was one victory by Celtic and one by Manchester United. Paisley's Liverpool celebrated the tenth anniversary of Celtic's success by winning in 1977. In the next season they marked the tenth anniversary of United's victory by retaining the trophy on the same Wembley pitch. In the two seasons after that, Brian Clough's Nottingham Forest won the biggest club trophy of all. Liverpool took it again in 1981 and Aston Villa did so in 1982. After a break in 1983 when Liverpool went out in the quarter-final to Widzew Lodz – the second leg was one of only two games the vastly influential Dalglish missed all season – they won it again a year later, under Joe Fagan. So, in seven seasons out of eight, an English club had been top of the heap. Who knows how much more success those clubs might have achieved but for the disaster of the 1985 final in Brussels which cost far more, in the end, than the original five-year ban? The domestic game suffered badly through those years of isolation from the best of the rest. Since the resumption of European fixtures, our clubs, almost without exception, have struggled to make much impact. We lost the impetus and a rising generation of players lost the opportunity to test themselves abroad, and to learn. We are still paying the price, no matter what heights of popularity football has reached since the advent of the Premiership, no matter how much money is now generated.

Paisley retired in 1983, before the Heysel blow descended. After being voted Manager of the Year six times, he rightly reckoned that he had done his bit and beyond it, and that he deserved to spend more time pottering around the house in the cardigan and slippers that had become his trademark. (On occasions he even wore the slippers at Anfield, to help ease the nagging from an old ankle injury.) Like Shankly he was awarded the OBE but unlike Shankly he became a director and general advisor on all things Liverpool until age and the illness that led to his death earlier this year forced him to stop. Ironically, his managerial career ended with Liverpool's worst run during his whole time in charge – five defeats and a draw in his last six games. But then they could risk Bob's wrath by taking things easily: they had won the title, again, with those six games to spare . . .

Joe Fagan, like Paisley a product of the Anfield boot-room, was next up for the job, and he amazed the football world by doing what every manager of an English club had, and has since, failed to do: he won *three* trophies in the first of his only two seasons in charge – the Championship (the third in a row, equal-ling the feats of Huddersfield in the 1920s and Arsenal in the 1930s), League Cup (in a replay against Everton) and European Champions Cup (after a pen-alty shoot-out against Roma) – and there could have been another date at Wembley if Liverpool had not suffered a rare bad day and lost to Second Division Brighton in the fourth round of the FA Cup. Everton went on to win that competition and so completed a Merseyside clean sweep.

Fagan was even older than Paisley had been when he moved into the manager's office (sixty-two) and he had been very much a 'number two' all his soccer life. He had played for Liverpool Schoolboys but the war meant that his professional debut was delayed for seven years. After serving in the Navy as a wireless telegra-phist on fleet minesweepers he returned to the game and had some success as a Manchester City defender, but he had to retire early because of a broken leg. After some time in non-League soccer he became trainer at Rochdale, doing everything including stoking the boilers. Eventually manager Harry Catterick, later of Everton, recommended him to Shankly. Gradually Fagan worked his way up at Anfield and despite his age was the obvious choice when Paisley stepped down, leaving a very good squad behind. 'I wasn't one hundred per cent sure I wanted the job,' said Fagan (echoes of the man he had succeeded). 'But I owed it to myself to try. If I hadn't, I would never have known how good a manager I was.'

Keeping up the good work was not as difficult as it

might have been for a newcomer, but soccer management is full of pitfalls. Fagan, that wise old bird, did not slip very often. In that first season, 1983/4, the team played sixty-six matches and lost only seven, consistently executing the old maxim about playing it to a red shirt. The red shirt receiving most of the passes belonged to Rush, who scored forty-seven goals plus a penalty in the shoot-out against Roma, and was described by his boss as being in a class of his own as a finisher. And so say all of us. Unfortunately for Liverpool, the following season had to be played without Souness, whose not unnatural desire to cash in on his talents took him to Sampdoria not long after he had lifted the Champions Cup in Rome. John Wark from Ipswich fired in some spectacular goals, but replacing a player like Souness was next to impossible. The squad also hit a bad run of injuries, the sort of thing that afflicts all clubs from time to time, but was unusual at Anfield where 101 per cent fitness is the norm. Rush, Johnston, Alan Kennedy, Lee and new striker Paul Walsh all had lengthy spells out, and the team simply could not withstand the challenge of a very strong Everton side. League Cup defeat by Spurs preceded FA Cup defeat by Manchester United in a semi-final replay (United beat Everton in the final) and so Europe was the only possible prize left. Poor Fagan. He had announced that this was to be his last match and victory over Juventus in the final in Brussels would have been a fine way for him to go. Even defeat could have been a departure with honour. But defeat was preceded by the appalling carnage engendered by the riotous behaviour of a minority of followers on a night that left an everlasting stain on the club's name. The TV image of Fagan's distress as he left the plane at Speke the following day, and sobbed his way across the tarmac and out of football, lingers yet.

Fagan might not have had to do much other than tinker with an engine that usually ran smoothly, but even so his record over his two seasons was remarkable: 129 games in major competitions, seventy outright victories plus one shoot-out, thirty-six draws and only twenty-two defeats, 225 goals scored and ninety-four conceded. Those are figures your average manager dreams about, yet Fagan's inheritance had been such that few people seemed to believe he had achieved anything out of the ordinary. He had in fact decided to go while his second season still had three months to run. 'I felt that the club needed new ideas and I had lost impetus. But there was never any pressure on me to go. The decision was mine.' The only parts of the job Fagan disliked, until those last awful hours, were media conferences and dropping players. But that did not stop him from dropping some, even Dalglish. 'What a daft devil I was,' he said. Fagan was then speaking in one of the very rare interviews he has given since his retirement. Like Paisley, and Shankly before them, Fagan still lives in a modest house near the ground, but has little contact with football. The cruel ending to his career ill became an honourable man.

Fagan left Anfield disillusioned with parts of society and did not presume to offer advice to his successor, Dalglish. He said he would not interfere, taking the view that the new boss could manage without an old one getting under his boots. 'Kenny has ability and good sense and can control the players,' Fagan said around the time that Dalglish took over. 'He is a young man [only thirty-four at the time of the appointment] and he deserves his chance. I'm sure he'll do well.' Dalglish certainly did: better than anybody had a right to expect. For a man with no previous managerial experience to achieve the record he achieved was remarkable then, after Ronnie Moran's brief spell as caretaker, Graeme Souness became Liverpool manager in April 1991. He remained in the job until January 1994, when he at last resigned, two days after Bristol City had knocked Liverpool out of the FA Cup, at Anfield, becoming the third team from a lower division to eject a Souness squad from a major competition in the space of three years: Bolton had done so, also at Anfield, in the previous season (the first home FA Cup defeat since 1964), and Peterborough had done so in a League Cup tie on their own ground not long after Souness had taken charge.

These were the most memorable of many upsets on the field, but to my mind there was an even worse manifestation of the malaise that had taken a grip of the club. Despite spending huge sums (the total deficit on his buying and selling was almost £10m), Souness's Liverpool not only lost far too many matches, they played far too often in a spirit of snarling aggression that mocked the excellent reputation for fair play assiduously built up over so many seasons. Liverpool teams always have had a nucleus of hard men, and rightly so. Football is a tough game. 'It's not for fairies or faint hearts,' Shankly said. Players I can name at random, such as Liddell, Tommy Smith, Yeats, Byrne, Moran, Lindsay and Case, were physically very strong and never less than one hundred per cent committed. Souness, too, was in that mould. Keegan was no giant but was superbly built. In the time-honoured phrase, they all got stuck in. But Liverpool rarely caused referees much bother. It is a remarkable statistic that not one Anfield player was sent off between 1939 and 1955 and, though rule changes have made that penalty much easier to incur, dismissals involving Liverpool players have remained pretty rare. Under Souness, however, that changed. McMahon and Ablett were sent off in the first few weeks of Souness's first full season, 1991/2. In the following season, in what proved to be the last three of the twelve European games the club played under the Souness regime, Stewart, Grobbelaar and Marsh were dismissed in turn (during the 144 pre-Souness European matches, many of them against niggling, obstructive opposition, Lawrenson and Dalglish had been the only men sent off, and Lawrenson still swears that he never touched the man he was alleged to have fouled). Redknapp followed just before Christmas in a 1–5 thrashing at Coventry – the first five-goal concession for seventeen years – and James and Hutchison were ordered from the field in successive fixtures late in the season. In 1993/4, Rob Jones emulated Redknapp by being first to the showers at Coventry, the ninth and thankfully the last before Souness left.

This awful record, I'm sure, was as upsetting to fans as were the frequent poor playing performances. And were they poor! Under Souness, Liverpool played 157 competitive games, won sixty-six, drew forty-six and lost forty-five. They finished sixth in both his two full seasons, and eighth in 1993/4, having been fifth at the time he left rather more than halfway through the programme. Many clubs would be happy with that but this was Liverpool, and this was not good enough. True, Liverpool won the FA Cup in 1992, but they made hard work of it: they needed a replay and extra time to eliminate Second Division Ipswich, and a last-minute goal in extra time, a replay, more extra time and then penalties to dispose of another team from Division Two, Portsmouth, in the semi-final. Poor Pompey: they gave their all for four hours, were never behind against a club whose very name used to scare opponents into submission, and still did not win. In the final, Liverpool looked anything but sure of victory over a mediocre Sunderland outfit until a thunderous volley from Michael Thomas, as superbly struck as it was unexpected, lightened their load. A second from Rush, his record-breaking fifth in three FA Cup final appearances, ensured that Mark Wright would lift the trophy.

As for the return to Europe, only three of the six teams Liverpool faced in two campaigns had any pretensions to class, and Liverpool's record against them was abysmal: five defeats, one victory. They did well to recover from 0–2 in France to beat Auxerre 3–0 in the second leg, on something akin to the Anfield glory nights that used to be taken for granted, but they lost both legs to Spartak Moscow, and were totally eclipsed in both legs against Genoa – two clubs in their centenary season – a year later. Earlier, they had even lost a second leg 0–1 to Finnish side Kuusysi Lahti, on a night when the Liverpool squad had so many injuries that they could barely raise a team.

When Souness eventually left, the defeat by Bristol City that pushed him over the edge was the club's first in thirteen games. But he had long overstayed his welcome. The board, who had seemed certain to sack him at the end of the previous season but surprisingly voted in favour of his retention, now agreed that he must go. The earlier decision to keep him, rather than pay off the remainder of his contract, was widely criticised on Merseyside – where a huge majority of callers to a radio poll wanted him out – and elsewhere. The board had allowed Souness to squander millions of pounds on a string of poor-to-average players. They had presided over a change of playing style that had led to more physical involvement (i.e. tackling and being tackled) that in turn led to huge numbers of injuries and the regrettable increase in clashes with opponents and red cards from referees. They had engaged Souness even though he had been involved in various suspensions and bans from the touchline during his managerial career in Scotland, and his excellent record as a player now counted for nothing. He had proved an unwise choice and the board, notably chairman David Moores, who had been his manager's number one supporter, stood condemned –

and still stand condemned – for not replacing Souness sooner than they did. A man given free rein at a football club can do a lot of harm in thirty-three months. While in charge at Anfield, Souness signed fourteen professionals from other clubs, at a total cost of more than £18m. As time passed and success obstinately stayed away from his door, he grew to rely too much on money to try to solve the club's problems.

I would rate only one of those fourteen signings, Rob Jones at £600,000 from Crewe, as a bargain, although Mark Wright (Derby) and Stig Bjornebye (Rosenborg Trondheim) have been particularly unlucky with injuries and so should be given the benefit of the doubt. David James cost £1m from Watford, a lot of money for a goalkeeper, but may yet prove to be worth it. The same applies to Neil Ruddock, although at £2.5m from Spurs he should be a better player than he is, no matter how the Koppites love him – he is nearing thirty and unlikely to get any faster. Of the others, Dean Saunders from Derby and Nigel Clough from Forest sometimes looked the part, more often did not. Paul Stewart, surprisingly, gained three England caps before joining Liverpool for £2.3m from Spurs; just over three years later, having been dropped several times and farmed out on loan to various lesser clubs, Stewart was given a free transfer. The same applied to Mark Walters, who had looked a good winger at Villa. Souness signed him for Rangers, then signed him again for Liverpool, at £1.25m. Walters, having Everton for a middle name, was perhaps doomed to fail after he turned up across the park from

Goodison. Michael Thomas sparked off the Wembley win over Sunderland, having gone to Anfield from Arsenal, but has done little since although injuries have again played a part. Lee Jones from Wrexham was bought for £300,000; if you cost that out per first-team game, he set Liverpool back £300,000 per match. Istvan Kozma, a Hungarian international, suddenly appeared from Dunfermline, made three full appearances plus six as substitute, and went home to Budapest for nothing (£300,000 less than he cost). Torben Piechnik was bought for £500,000 and was back in Denmark inside two years having achieved slightly more than absolute zero. Is it any surprise that fans are bemused by transfers like that?

Saunders was the only player Souness signed and then sold while at Liverpool; he was sent to Aston Villa (and Liverpool lost £500,000 on the deal). Of those inherited from the Dalglish days, Souness also sold Steve Staunton and Ray Houghton to Villa, Peter Beardsley and Gary Ablett to Everton, Barry Venison to Newcastle, Steven McMahon to Manchester City and Ronny Rosenthal to Spurs. As luck would have it, these men flourished at their new clubs: Saunders and Staunton helped Villa to win the League Cup and Houghton, although only a sub in that final, did well with the Republic of Ireland in the 1994 World Cup, scoring the goal that beat Italy. Beardsley had a good spell with Everton before returning to Newcastle and regaining an England place when he might have expected a bus pass. Ablett became the first player ever to win the FA Cup with both Merseyside clubs. Venison too got into the England team. McMahon eventually became player-manager at Swindon and Rosenthal, unpredictable as ever, scored some sensational goals for Spurs. Apart from goalkeeper Mike Hooper, who was unable to match the competition at Newcastle, and Jimmy Carter, who disappeared into a hole at Highbury just as big as the one he fell into at Anfield, all these players earned ticks instead of crosses.

Then there was Julian Dicks, a rough, tough fullback who came from West Ham in an exchange deal, with David Burrows and Mike Marsh going to London. Dicks started twenty-eight games for Liverpool, scoring three goals, and then, after Souness had left, was transferred back to the Hammers. He was no loss. Although Dicks did not cost Liverpool a fee, he became yet another in the list of ill-judged signings. But Souness let himself down too. You can forgive him to some extent for his transfer deals, because we all make mistakes. You can forgive him to some extent for the over-emphasis on the physical side of the game, and for his own well-documented rows with officialdom, because he was under great pressure to succeed in his avowed intention of 'returning the club to their former glory' (although they had not gone without their share of glory even in the latter days of Dalglish). You can forgive him for sacking that tremendous Anfield stalwart, Phil Thompson, as second-team coach, because any boss will want to recruit his own staff. You can only admire him for his courage in carrying out his duties before and after his heart bypass operation shortly before the 1992 Wembley appearance. But you cannot forgive him for selling his story of that particular part of his life to the *Sun*, a tabloid widely despised on Merseyside for its appallingly inaccurate coverage of the Hillsborough disaster. Three years had gone by since then, to the exact day, when the Souness story appeared, complete with the sort of photographs of the patient and his girlfriend, later to become his second wife, that the *Sun* considers appropriate in such circumstances. Merseyside was horrified. Most of footballing Britain, I imagine, felt the same way. This crass insensitivity, by the paper's executives as well as by Souness, caused widespread outrage. An apology by Souness, and the donation of his fee to a children's hospital, was nowhere near enough compensation. From that moment, there was only one place for Souness as far as the overwhelming majority of one-time admirers was concerned, and that was outside Anfield's doors. He should have quit. When he did not, the board should have ensured that he did. Instead, the most depressing period of Liverpool FC's history was allowed to drag on for what seemed an eternity until at last, at long, long last, Souness did the right thing.

Roy Evans, yet another product of the bootroom that was no more – demolished to make way for improved media facilities – was the man chosen to take over, having been appointed assistant manager in the closing months of the Souness regime. Perhaps the board, like the fans, were hoping that a return to progression from within would mean a return to the good old days of title upon title. After all, the virtually seamless transition from Shankly to Paisley to Fagan to Dalglish had worked well enough. Evans had had a curious career as a player. He was an England school-boy international full-back from Bootle but played only eleven senior games for Liverpool – not much more than one a season – before deciding to retire at the age of twenty-five and concentrate on coaching. He did the job so well that the Reds' reserves won the Central League title nine times in eleven years. Having so many good players left over when the first-team quota was full obviously helped to some extent, but there can be little doubt that Evans has the knack of helping youngsters on their way, by example as well as by advice. He is quietly spoken, not given to smashing cups and upsetting the tea urn, although I believe he can hold his own in a shouting match. And he certainly knows how to wave a chequebook about: in less than two years he spent more than £17m on Scales, Babb, Mark Kennedy from Millwall, reserve goalkeeper Michael Stensgaard from Danish club Hvidovre, and Collymore from Forest for what was then Britain's biggest fee. Even allowing for the inflationary spiral that affects football at irregular periods, these were really big deals, and all these signings need time before they can be judged successes or failures.

Evans certainly needed to do something to rejuven-ate the dispirited bunch of players he inherited, but consistency was hard to establish. Liverpool twice had to come from behind to draw at Norwich in his first match, were four down in the Southampton snow before salvaging pride (if no points) with two late goals, then lost 0–2 at Leeds. A first-minute goal by Rush

against Coventry, then managed by Phil Neal, got
Evans his first win, which was followed by a 0–2 defeat
at Dalglish's Blackburn and a 2–1 home win against
the old foes, Everton. This, the 150th local derby
and the last before the Kop's demise, was notable for
a splendid winner from young Fowler after Watson and
Rush had scored within thirty seconds of each other.
It was also notable for kicking off at five p.m. on a
Sunday because the lords of Sky TV decreed it should
be so. If the fans were consulted, I did not hear of it.

And so the in-and-out Evans progress went on to
the end of the season at which point his sixteen games
in charge had produced only five wins, two draws and
nine defeats, fifteen goals scored, twenty-three conceded and twenty-three players used. There was a press-
ing need to buy. No longer could the manager say, as
Shankly would when asked what his team would be,
'Same as last season.' Evans brought some money in
by selling Dicks back to West Ham and getting them
to take Don Hutchison as well. Hutchison had hung
about for four years or so, rarely appearing in the team
and too often appearing in the tabloids. (Herbert
Chapman, the legendary manager who took Arsenal to
greatness before the war, is reputed to have pulled out
of a proposed signing when he saw the player concerned eating peas off his knife. I wonder what Chapman would have thought about Hutchison?)
Grobbelaar went, to Southampton, and Whelan and
Nicol left on free transfers, Whelan to become player-
manager of Southend and Nicol as player-coach at
Notts County and then to Sheffield Wednesday, with a

narrow escape from drowning in a flooded gravel pit in between.

The Evans rebuilding began to show results. Not only did Liverpool climb the table to fourth, they also won the Coca-Cola Cup giving the manager a trophy in his first full season. An unusual formation of three backs, five in midfield and the Rush-Fowler tandem up front baffled plenty of opponents, with the defence showing something of the ironclad appearance taken for granted in previous seasons. Barnes appeared rejuvenated after a depressing run of injuries, and Rush continued to defy the ageing process. Best of all, as far as the future was concerned, Fowler, Redknapp and McManaman were fully settled. Gates picked up, with the rebuilt stadium usually close to capacity, and success in both Cup competitions compensated for absence from Europe.

For a time there were hopes of two appearances at Wembley in the same season but three days after qualification for the first final was assured (thanks to a Fowler goal against Crystal Palace), Spurs claimed a rare victory at Anfield in the sixth round of the FA Cup. Jurgen Klinsmann scored the vital goal during his first and last season in England in which he was voted Footballer of the Year and which, in the way of the modern superstar, he completed by going home to Bayern Munich and a new, better contract. This defeat was only the second in a spell of twenty-five games, and Klinsmann's goal came just when everybody must have been expecting Liverpool to draw for the fourth round in succession. They won in a shoot-out in round three after two draws with Birmingham (who put three penalties wide and had one saved by James), then beat Burnley 1–0 after a 0–0 at Turf Moor, and won 2–0 away to Wimbledon after being held 1–1 in front of the all-seater Kop. The victory over Burnley was only Liverpool's second outright win in the previous eleven FA Cup games, all of them against clubs from lower divisions, although two others had been won on penalties.

Progress in the Coca-Cola Cup was much more satisfying. All eight games were won at the first attempt and the build-up to Wembley included a Rush hat-trick at Blackburn (his 600th appearance for the club), a Rush winner against Arsenal, and 1–0 victories over Crystal Palace in both legs of the semi-final. Incidentally, Liverpool achieved the odd distinction of beating different clubs on the same ground in successive matches in different competitions, in the course of visiting Selhurst Park six times during the season without losing once. They beat Palace 6–1 there on the opening day of the season in August, had a League game with Wimbledon rained off in January, had the Coca-Cola Cup game postponed for the same reason in February, beat Wimbledon 2–0 in the FA Cup a week later, won the restaged Coca-Cola game against Palace ten days after that, and drew 0–0 with Wimbledon in May. The highlights of this curious season included that opening thrashing of Palace; a 3–0 home defeat of Arsenal in the next game, with Fowler getting all three in an official time of four minutes thirty-three seconds; and splendid 2–0 victories over title contenders Newcastle and Manchester United in March on either side of a 2–3 defeat by Coventry (when Peter Ndlovu became the first visiting player to score a hat-trick at Anfield since 1962). Then there was the curious and marvellously exciting last afternoon when Dalglish's Blackburn, on Dalglish's old ground, lost to a last-minute goal by Dalglish's last signing, Jamie Redknapp, but still took the Premiership title by a point because Manchester United could only draw at West Ham.

Earlier, however, there had been that trip to Wembley, still a great occasion – and all the more so for those of the younger generation unaccustomed to watching Liverpool there as often as we did in the days when the Charity Shield was the first home game of the season and the FA Cup final the last. Second Division Bolton were the opponents in the Coca-Cola Cup final and an excellent match it was, decided by two individual goals from McManaman, only just twenty-three but turning on a fine display. He comprehensively trumped Bolton's aces, McAteer and McGinlay, but the former's form throughout the season was enough to persuade Evans to add him to the Anfield strength later in the year. Bolton's rally to halve the deficit added to the thrills and showed that Liverpool still had some way to go to regain their old eminence, but nevertheless Evans became the fourth successive Liverpool manager to win a trophy in his first full season, the Coca-Cola Cup medal, his first individual honour since 1973 when he took a sabbatical from his first love and helped Philadelphia Atoms to the North American

Soccer League title. Obviously he realises that he has a lot more to do, and the pressures are enormous: a club with such a reputation for success must be even harder to manage than one with no past form. The weight of expectation in this somewhat saddened city, too, must be cruel, and after two years in the job Evans appeared to have aged considerably. Perhaps it was my imagination, but he turned rather younger again during 1995/6, a generally excellent season which brought a rise to third place and a run to the FA Cup Final. The smiles would have been back on Anfield faces to an even greater extent but for a dire November, when six games brought a draw and five defeats, by Brondby in the Uefa Cup, by Kevin Keegan's Newcastle in both Premiership and Coca-Cola Cup, by Everton at home and by Middlesbrough away. The season from then on comprised another thirty games, of which Liverpool lost only three! Rush broke the twentieth-century FA Cup record by scoring his forty-second goal in the competition, and Fowler's remarkable total of thirty-six goals included at least one in every round before the final, two against Manchester United away in the League and two more at home. Not surprisingly, Fowler could not score against them for a third time, at Wembley, where a remarkably dull game – between teams costing more than £30 million in transfer fees, remember – was decided by a late goal from Cantona, virtually a reformed character on his return from suspension for assaulting a spectator.

Liverpool, badly let down in certain positions on the day, did not deserve to win. And they know that creating a team to do a long-term matching job on United, with their enormous revenue and some excellent trawlers hauling in their young catches, is going to be dreadfully difficult. We can only wish Evans well as he goes about the task.

Chapter Five
King Kenny

On the day Kenny Dalglish joined Liverpool from Celtic he was twenty-six and looked sixteen. On the day he left he had just turned forty and looked to be approaching sixty. In between, Dalglish had enchanted crowds wherever he had gone, become a millionaire, more than doubled an already remarkable collection of footballing honours, survived two appalling disasters to add to the one he had experienced in Glasgow, and become the most influential character in Liverpool FC history. Shankly was a larger-than-life personality who revived the club and led the way to some marvellous feats. Paisley's record was even better. Yet Dalglish outstripped both in terms of the cumulative effect, what he achieved off the field as well as on.

As far as the game is concerned, Dalglish was born lucky. He was a wonderful player, lucky to play for two highly successful clubs, and lucky to be surrounded by excellent colleagues throughout his career. As a manager, he was lucky to be with one wealthy club, Liverpool, whose finances were later dwarfed by the multi-millionaire Jack Walker of Blackburn Rovers. Whether

Dalglish would have had the success on the field had he begun with Raith Rovers or Stenhousemuir is a question without a definitive answer, though his talent was such that surely he would have gone to a big club while still young enough to learn. As a manager, his path was smoothed by having money to spend: I doubt whether Blackburn would have gained promotion (via a desperate struggle through the play-offs in 1992) without Walker's cash, let alone won 1995's Premiership title. Yet that perhaps is to decry his ability as a judge of players. Even Shankly and Paisley made some poor buys while at Anfield, and Dalglish's record as a marketeer was generally a good one, marred only in the final months.

Dalglish also seems to be well blessed with a family life kept as private as can be, given the circumstances of his goldfish-bowl existence. But only he can possibly know the appalling strain he was put under in the three footballing tragedies that affected him. The first was in 1971, when Dalglish was only nineteen. He had gone to Ibrox Park to watch the traditional New Year game between Rangers and Celtic, when sixty-six people were suffocated and many more injured. Fourteen years later, as Dalglish was poised to succeed the retiring Joe Fagan and become Liverpool's player-manager, the Heysel tragedy engulfed the departing boss, his successor, the team, the club, the fans and the entire football world. The choice of Dalglish as player-manager at England's number one club was controversial, to say the least. How much more of a trial did it become, I wonder, because of the circumstances in which he came to inherit? Then, four years on, came Hillsborough, where so many more people perished simply because they followed their love of soccer to the wrong place at the wrong time. Dalglish was then thirty-eight, no great age for a man to be involved in such a heart-rending welter of funerals and memorials and hospital visits, all the while trying to keep the club afloat. He and his wife earned enormous respect and gratitude for what they did in those harrowing weeks.

Eventually, in February 1991, Dalglish quit, knocking the Gulf War off the front pages with a sensation greater even than Shankly's decision to step down seventeen years earlier. The team's 4–4 draw in that remarkable replayed FA Cup tie at Everton had been acclaimed as one of the greatest football matches ever seen (ever seen on television, which is not the same thing) but it had pushed Dalglish over the edge. For the first time in living memory, Liverpool failed to win a match after leading four times. Even after giving Everton due credit for their refusal to submit, it was a dire failure on the part of Dalglish's defence that helped lead to his decision. He said he was worn out, and he certainly looked it. He said that for the first time since he took the job, he was putting Kenny Dalglish before the club and the team. And then he was gone. There has been any amount of speculation about the 'real' reason why Dalglish quit a team who were then top of the First Division and still in the FA Cup pending the second replay with Everton. Why not accept that the decision was simply as its maker said it was? He was tired and could no longer cope with the pressure that was making his life a misery.

Eight months later, and looking years younger, Dalglish came back, to take up another less stressful but still demanding appointment. He has done well at Blackburn, too, winning yet another Championship before taking a supervisory role, although he may well have to wait a long, long time before Rovers can recruit a team showing the consistency of his old Liverpool outfits. He might even quit again, although football must be in his blood to such an extent that I doubt if he could be away from it for long. Whatever he does, he will go his own way. Dalglish is, always was, his own man. A superstitious one, as well. He would never captain a team because he would never go out on the pitch first. Even when player-manager at Anfield, he let players such as Hansen and Whelan act as captain. When he was monopolising the Manager of the Month award, the prize being a cheque and a gallon of Scotland's best-known product, the public relations officer for the distillery had to present the goodies during the pre-match kickabout: Dalglish would not go out alone to collect them. He always went to bed on Friday afternoons, even leaving early when a guest of honour at celebrity lunches, and on Friday mornings he made the rest of the squad join him in a ceremonial choccy bikky, always distributed by the same YTS lad.

Dalglish signed for Celtic when sixteen years and two months old, a couple of weeks before the club's European Cup win over Inter Milan in Lisbon. As a boy, and a Protestant boy at that, he had supported

Rangers; he, his parents and sister lived in a flat over-looking the club's training ground. He had played for Scotland's under-16 team, but Rangers ignored him. One theory put forward for this lapse was that a scout sent to interview him went to the home of another Dalglish family by mistake. Their door opened to reveal lighted candles beneath a picture of the Virgin Mary, whereupon the scout made his excuses and left, never to return. Jock Stein signed him for Celtic in return for a £200 donation to his junior club, which might just rank as the best £200 any manager has ever spent. The boy played only two senior games in his first season at Parkhead, and three in his second, but after-wards he had such an impact that he made his full debut for Scotland, in a European Championship qualifying game against Belgium, after only sixteen first-team appearances. Even earlier, he had been in the under-23 team and scored twice in a 2–2 draw against an England side with a debutant of their own: Kevin Keegan. Dalglish was even then showing ability in vari-ous roles: winger, midfield, even striker. When Stein was asked about the lad's best position, he replied: 'Och, just toss him a shirt and let him out.'

In six full seasons with Celtic, Dalglish won nine medals – four for the League, four for the Scottish Cup and one for the League Cup, with the club losing in the final in all his other five years. He had become as big a hero on Clydeside as Keegan had on Mersey-side, so a succession of one by the other seemed the obvious answer once Keegan opted for Hamburg. 'Money doesn't come into it,' was the Dalglish credo at the time, despite rumours that he needed a signing-on fee to help with a family business venture. Bob Paisley was called back from holiday to help in the negotiations, and said later: 'All done in ten minutes. No haggling, no bartering. We wanted Kenny and he wanted to come to us. He was the best signing ever, as well. Right from the start he could read my team. He understood them better than they understood him, and that's the hallmark of a great player.' Liverpool changed their style somewhat to accommodate him, with more ball-to-feet passing than the ball-to-head which had led to so many goals for the Toshack-Keegan alliance, and Dalglish went on to become the most influential of all the many stringpullers I have seen in my years as a Red. Although of moderate height he had great strength in his legs, and was notoriously hard to dispossess. I have never seen a better player with his back to the opposing goal. In addition, he was genuinely two-footed, good with his head, cool under pressure and blessed with that instinct for goals that all great strikers have. Add a steely determination to succeed, and all the ingredients for success were there. His only fault of any noticeable size was his desire to referee games as well as play in them – 'He's the moaningest minnie I've ever met in football,' said John Bond, with perhaps more than a touch of sour grapes. Dalglish also had occasional rushes of blood. Against Benfica in 1984, for example, he got himself sent off, fortunately taking an opponent with him, after an exchange of blows. This was when Liverpool were under the cosh, only 3–2 ahead on aggregate with half the game to go and an away goal conceded in the first leg. Fortunately, Grobbelaar, Neal and the rest did the necessary and protected the lead. Generally speaking, Dalglish comported himself excellently on the field, and even opposing fans might have indulged in a wry smile when he scored against them, such was the child-like delight he showed at such successes.

He had not been on Merseyside long before he was known everywhere, in contrast to his arrival. A few days after signing, he was able to walk the near-mile length of Lord Street in Southport unapproached and to treat his wife and children in an ice-cream shop, totally ignored. Such bliss did not last, and he was soon an object of huge interest. But he was nearly always polite and straightforward, even joking at the expense of his accent, which Mike Langley had described as making him sound like a strangulated Billy Connolly. Dalglish used that line in his speech of thanks after being named Footballer of the Year, as he was in 1979 and 1983, to go with the PFA award in 1983, and Manager of the Year in 1986, 1988 and 1990 at Anfield and 1995 at Ewood, as well as receiving the MBE and Freedom of the City of Glasgow. By then he had played for Scotland a record 102 times, out of a possible 140, in a period of almost fifteen years. He appeared in three World Cups, which would have become four, even at the age of thirty-five, but for an injury keeping him out of the squad for Mexico in 1986. His thirty goals equalled the Scottish record set by Denis Law – one of his boyhood heroes – and although I know Scots who say he was often a disap-

pointment when wearing his country's shirt, he had
many magnificent moments. Who could forget his
header late on in a frenetic World Cup qualifier against
Wales at Anfield in 1978?

Club matches seemed to suit Dalglish more than
internationals, and his record gets better the more you
look at it. While winning his nine medals with Celtic
he made 323 competitive appearances and scored 167
goals. With Liverpool his figures were 496 and 168,
making him the only player to collect a century of
goals for a single club in each country, and all of them
in the top division. As player and manager with Liverpool he won eight Championship medals, two for the
FA Cup, three for the European Champions Cup and
four for the League Cup, plus such incidentals as the
European Super Cup and the ScreenSport Super Cup,
a made-for-TV mini-competition in the days before
Murdoch woke up to football and the authorities and
the terrestrial channels were wrangling over peanuts.
He followed Joe Mercer and became the second man
to win both League and Cup as player and manager
(George Graham later achieved this double), and when
he won the Premiership with Blackburn he became
only the third manager, after Herbert Chapman and
Brian Clough, to win the top division's trophy with
different clubs. One little-known achievement to Dalglish's credit is that, including replays and two-legged
affairs, he appeared in sixteen major Cup finals for
Liverpool in succession. That run started against Nottingham Forest in 1978, when he missed an open goal
in the first minute of a 0–0 League Cup draw – Forest

won the replay with a disputed penalty – and ended in
1987, when he went on as an ineffective substitute in a
1–2 League Cup defeat by Arsenal, the first goal being
scored by Nicholas with his left heel and the second
being scored by Nicholas with his right thigh. The
only other defeats in this sequence of Cup finals, which
included eight wins and three draws, had been by
unusually useful opponents: Flamengo of Brazil in the
1982 World Cup Championship, Independiente of
Argentina in the same competition in 1985, and Juventus at Heysel.

Eventually the time came for Dalglish to step down
as a player. Then, after being one of the lads in the
dressing-room, and a widely popular one, his dry
humour contrasting with that serious outward manner,
he had to take a somewhat different attitude. Like
Shankly, Paisley and Fagan, he had to show that he
was in charge. A difficult stance for him to adopt after
such a time, and difficult too for the others, particularly
Chris Lawler, then coaching the reserves, and Geoff
Twentyman, the scout whose prize captures had
included Heighway, Rush and Nicol. Both these fine
club servants went, unhappily, as Dalglish set about
building his own empire. It seemed to work pretty well
apart from those awful anti-climaxes against Wimbledon at Wembley and in the title decider against Arsenal
in the following year, when the team appeared desper-
ately short of motivation and, surprising though it may
seem in matches with such high stakes, commitment.

After a lengthy period with only one big signing,
McMahon, Dalglish brought in several newcomers

who seemed highly expensive: Barnes, Beardsley, Ald-ridge and Houghton cost about £4m between them, Burrows, Spackman and Venison another million or so. Rush came back from Italy for nearly £3m, although he had brought in more when he went, a year earlier. Only Staunton, snapped up from Dundalk, came for a small sum. Later, Hysen and Rosenthal arrived from abroad, neither of them doing well enough to be called bargains, as the others had been. And then, as the post-Hillsborough strain surely began to tell, Dalglish bought the controversial Speedie and the unimpressive Carter, failures both, and – just to show that his judge-ment had not gone entirely haywire – he signed the seventeen-year-old Redknapp. Very few good local products appeared while Dalglish ran the show, but by then all the big clubs were becoming more and more reliant on buying players to make the wheels go round. He had money to spend, and generally he spent it wisely. Money, I believe, is a subject close to Dalglish's heart. He certainly was paid an enormous amount during his spell on Merseyside, but if anyone can be said to have earned such sums, he could. His salary and bonuses, in the later period, must have been around £250,000 a year, supplemented by football-related items such as advertising and videos. He also copped for two benefits, one from a match against Real Socie-dad in 1990 that grossed more than £150,000, and the other in Scotland four years earlier, organised by well-wishers. This brought in £60,000, which Dalglish was content to leave invested, earning high interest: he did not need it for any immediate purpose. Both events had followed Inland Revenue guidelines and 'had been organised by volunteer committees in which the beneficiary played no part'. How a man cannot play some part, however small, in his own testimonial is beyond me, but the taxman seemed happy. So too did Dalglish and his supporters, leaving successive Chancellors of the Exchequer as the only people with a grouse. Now, only a few years later, the Ruddocks and the Collymores are being paid (not necessarily earning) amounts far beyond our Ken.

At the time Dalglish left Anfield, he had been in top football for nineteen full seasons with two clubs and had won twenty-six major trophies, including eight doubles and a treble; in only three of those seasons (one in Scotland, two in England) had he failed to win anything. All a bit difficult to take in, so look at it in figures. Starting from his first full season, 1971/2, up to and including his last, 1989/90, the number of trophies he won was: 2–1–2–2–0–2 in Scotland, and 1–1–1–2–2–2–3–0–2–0–1–1–1 in England. These are wins, remember. In addition, during his time Celtic were second once and third once in the League, lost in one Scottish Cup final and in five League Cup finals. After his arrival at Anfield, Liverpool were League runners-up four times, losing FA Cup finalists once and semi-finalists four times, losing League Cup finalists twice and semi-finalists once, and losing European Champions Cup finalists once. So his amazing total of successes could have been even greater. If the £200 Stein gave for Dalglish was the greatest bargain ever, the £440,000 Liverpool paid for him was almost as much of a steal, even though it was then the British record fee. Yet they could have had him for nothing at fifteen, after he had written to the club for a trial. He duly travelled down and played for a junior team against Southport reserves; I know a man who saw it. 'We'll let you know,' the lad was told, but he heard nothing more (unlike Alan Hansen a little later, who had a 'Thanks but no thanks' letter within days).

Dalglish was a great player, possibly second only to Best among all those produced in Britain since the war. He was – is – a pretty effective manager. And he is, and always will be, renowned for his effect on the game in general and on two great clubs in particular.

Chapter Six
Simply the best:
the all-time XI

First: Dalglish. Second: Rush. Third: Souness. Those names, I guess, would be the first to be pencilled, inked, typed or word-processed in when picking a Greatest Ever Liverpool XI.

I cannot imagine anyone making a case for leaving out any of the three. Dalglish? The best British footballer since Best and worth a chapter of his own in this book. Rush? If you had to back a man to score a goal when your life depended on it, surely he would be your choice. Souness? Forget the moneybags manager, this is the clockmaker to make the rest tick. As if they needed any winding up. So that's the first three; now the problems start. You can pick a team from all the hundreds of men who have played for all the Liverpool teams down all those years since September 1892 when the first of all those competitive matches was staged. You can assume that everybody is in prime physical condition, mentally attuned, and at the very peak of his form. But how do you make the comparisons? How can you relate players from the days before the Kop was built to those who go out in front of the present

Bill Shankly – the man who between 1959 and 1974 converted Liverpool into the strongest club side in Britain

Ronnie Moran, Kenny Dalglish and current
manager Roy Evans celebrate the 1990
Championship victory

European Cup winners for the
first time – Emlyn Hughes with the trophy
after Liverpool's classic 3-1 victory over
Borussia Munchengladbach

Bob Paisley holds aloft the championship trophy in 1983, his last year in charge of the club

has emerged as
Britain's brightest young striker after just
two seasons of Premiership football

These two goals from **Ian Rush**, in 1986 (above) and 1989,
helped Liverpool to win the Merseyside FA Cup Finals.

Ian Rush, Sammy Lee and Craig Johnston celebrate the 1984 penalties win over Roma which earned the club their fourth European Cup victory

Liverpool won the League and Cup "double" for the first time in 1986. Kenny Dalglish, in his first season as Player-Manager, scored the goal at Chelsea which clinched the championship

all-seater edifice? I believe that fans love picking teams, to liven up a journey to or from a match or to brighten an evening in pub or club. For better or worse, I have chosen the 'Big Three' of my 'Big Eleven'. Now I adjust my wig, tuck my thumbs in my waistcoat, clear my throat and try to put a case for the others. Difficult, m'lud? That word's not strong enough.

Number one is a good place to start. In the days when telegrams preceded the fax machine the club's telegraphic address was simply Goalkeeper, Liverpool . . . which gives you some idea of how well the goals were guarded. Sam Hardy had seven seasons at Anfield and an international career that lasted thirteen years, on either side of World War One. I have a book, written in 1937, that names Hardy as the greatest keeper of all, up to that stage in soccer history. But then there was Elisha Scott, Ireland's first choice for sixteen years and compiler of a then-record 467 senior games for the Reds. 'Leesh' was a legendary figure at a time when the team's form was rarely more than middling. Arthur Riley was pretty useful too, playing more than 300 matches before the war interrupted proceedings. Then came Welshman Cyril Sidlow, and Cockney Dave Underwood, and South African Doug Rudham, and the big boy from Edinburgh, Tommy Younger, eventually followed by another Scot, Bert Slater, and another, Tommy Lawrence. The fans called Tommy 'The Flying Pig' (perhaps he *was* a bit overweight) but after he had waited five years to get into the first team, something extraordinary happened. Shankly arrived and saw things others could not see.

Result: Tommy the Porcine Pilot missed barely a match for seven seasons.

He was followed by Ray Clemence, one of Shankly's bargains and one-third of a quiz question: which three former Scunthorpe players have captained England? Clem and Kevin Keegan did so at soccer, Ian Botham at cricket. Clemence made 656 senior appearances for Liverpool and won fifty-six caps while there, plus another five when extending his career at Spurs after leaving Anfield in curious circumstances. He was a fine keeper and would be the first choice for many, but – we are taking everyone at the absolute peak of form – he let in two bum goals in two games when playing against Scotland and a certain K Dalglish. So I go for his successor, Bruce Grobbelaar. He was roundly decried for his frequent errors (not as frequent as all that, but most of them were, of course, shown on TV) but his sheer brilliance as an athlete gets him my vote. Watch the video of his save from Sharp's header at Wembley in 1986: what other keeper could have got there? Sadly, Brucie left Anfield under a cloud of smoke generated by clashes with Souness, and has since got into terrible trouble. But how did he go through his first five seasons without missing a match? How did he equal Clemence as English soccer's most decorated keeper (thirteen major domestic medals)? How did he become one of only seventeen players to feature in three winning Wembley FA Cup final teams? Playing behind a good defence helped, sure, but Brucie deserves a lot of credit for his efforts, too. (He was not, by the way, the first Liverpool personality to walk on his hands: manager Don Welsh could, even in middle age.) David James, the latest in the line of Anfield keepers, has a lot to do if he is to match Grobbelaar, Clemence and the rest.

Next, the back four. More like forty. When I go for Tommy Smith, Mark Lawrenson, Alan Hansen and Steve Nicol, that is not to disparage the others. How about Chris Lawler, Phil Thompson, Emlyn Hughes and Alex Lindsay for another foursome? Or Phil Neal, Mark Wright, Ron Yeats and Gerry Byrne? Or Rob Jones, John Scales, Gary Gillespie and Alan Kennedy? That's at least four top fours in the past thirty years, ignoring others such as Neil Ruddock and Larry Lloyd (a big man with several even bigger brothers), Steve 'sold too soon' Staunton, Gary Ablett (who was hammered by press and public but still became the only man to gain an FA Cup winner's medal with both Reds and Blues), the slow but classy Glenn Hysen, the versatile David Burrows, and Phil Babb, one-third of the recent, somewhat revolutionary, defensive line-up. There were some good guys around before then, too. Bill Jones (Rob's grandad) was a utility player, occupying seven positions in the days when numbers on shirts were there only to help the paying public, not to help the paying public *and* work as a marketing tool. He was England's centre-half twice in 1950 but failed to do himself justice. When he lost his place, clubmate Laurie Hughes stepped up for a three-match England 'career' that took in the 1950 World Cup in Brazil, but Hughes surely would have got a more extended run had it not been for a knee wrecked in a Charity

Shield game. Hughes played at Belo Horizonte when England lost 0–1 to the Americans. 'We could have played for a month and we wouldn't have scored,' he said. Ray Lambert, Eddie Spicer (who came back after one broken leg, but could not do the same after a second), Dick White and Ronnie Moran were other good club servants at various times in the first two decades after World War Two (this is the same Moran who has filled so many other Anfield roles since). Around the turn of the century there was Alex Raisbeck (of 'the rapid movement and fierce electrical rushes'); Ephraim Longworth, also way back, was the first Liverpool player to captain England; in the World War One era, there was Donald McKinlay; and then there were James 'Parson' Jackson, who dropped soccer to become a minister, and 'Tiny' Bradshaw, who won a single cap in 1928 and so became one of Scotland's 5–1 Wembley Wizards.

I pick Smith at right-back, as the position used to be called, in my Best Ever XI, because he has to go in somewhere. I cannot imagine my team lining up against Gods United, or Mars, or whoever, without Smith, that scowling lump of menace on legs. He could play, too, as well as being in there 'to rattle their bones', as Shankly put it. Smith is still the club's youngest ever FA Cup finalist, just twenty in 1965 when his attitude, as much as his power, put poor Albert Johanesson of Leeds out of the game from the start. A dozen years later 'the Anfield iron' was as big a giant as most of those winning the club's first European Champions Cup (but he missed the second a year later after dropping a pickaxe on his feet). Lawler and Neal, who must make way for Smith, were incredibly durable. A seven-year spell in which only one League game was missed was Lawler's record; Neal surpassed even that staggering feat by missing only one in *ten* seasons. Lawler scored sixty-one goals without a single penalty, Neal sixty with the aid of several. Remember Rome 1976? When was another penalty so perfectly placed? But Smith must go in.

Lawrenson was class, possibly even more so than Hansen. Both were wonderfully mobile for tall men, adept on the ball, moving through the maelstrom of the modern penalty area with grace oozing out of every pore, despite the considerable physical strain they were under (don't ask Hansen about his knees). Alan the Immaculate played football as well as he now talks it. As for Lorro, a few years ago, in Mullally's boozer behind the Mirror Group building, I told him that he was among my Liverpool all-time selection. 'Surely they must have had somebody better than me,' he replied. A wonderful player, and modest, too. Phil Thompson 'tossed up with a sparrow for his legs, and lost', said Shankly. If you are surprised to learn that he was capped forty-two times, don't be: England have had few better. And what a Red, from top to toe. Emlyn Hughes upset half of Merseyside on his return from Rome in 1977 with his bubbly-inspired 'Liverpool are magic, Everton are tragic' blurt into a TV mike (he had the good sense to apologise), but he was a wonderful buy for Liverpool, seemingly impervious to injury (a trait possibly inherited from his dad, a

rugby league international) and with limitless enthusiasm to atone for his lack of the skill that made my
first choices my first choices. Much-travelled Scouse
Ron Atkinson is known as Big Ron for his size as
well as his deals, but there was only one Big Ron
as far as Anfield is concerned: the enormous
Yeats, who defended as well as any players could when
they were so one-footed, and enlivened the odd attack
by charging up and heading goals like a hammer
knocking in a nail. Mark Wright has done well to
return from nasty injuries (including a leg broken when
playing for Southampton against Liverpool), had a
good World Cup in 1990, and has had a resurgence at
club level as well. Gillespie gained thirteen caps for
Scotland, a number that symbolised his ill luck with
injuries and illness, as when he missed Wembley in
1986.

Left-back is another close-run thing, and only Steve
Nicol's all-round ability puts him ahead of one of my
Liverpool favourites, Alec Lindsay, he of the educated
left foot and the penchant for reading *Shooting Times*.
He should be in the record books after shooting one
of Wembley's greatest goals, but was robbed by an
incorrect decision favouring Newcastle in 1974. Lindsay took the ball off an opponent, raced forward,
played it inside towards Keegan, then hit the return
like a bullet, finding a fine angle, past the keeper.
'Offside,' said Gordon Kew, thinking that Keegan had
played a wall pass. In fact, KK had let the ball run past
him, and a rebound off the defender was the last touch
before Lindsay's tremendous blast. Mr Kew admitted

he was wrong after he had seen the video, and the result was unaffected, but I still feel sorry for Lindsay. Nicol was Footballer of the Year in 1989, when he had to bear the extra crosses of so many post-Hillsborough funerals. He had the adaptability needed in the modern game (once scoring a hat-trick at Newcastle when nominally playing in defence), and used those enormous feet to exercise considerable ball skill.

Many a Koppite would want Gerry Byrne, who was one of their own, in the Top Team. I saw him make his senior debut, at Charlton, all those years ago, when he put through his own goal in a 1–5 thumping. 'I'll get over it,' he sighed, as we trudged back to Euston. Gerry did, too, although he took a while to emulate George Hardwick, who had the same unfortunate start and went on to play for England. Nearly a decade after Charlton's Valley of Despair, Byrne was an FA Cup final hero, playing 117 minutes out of 120 against Leeds after trainer Bob Paisley had told him his collar-bone was bust. I don't know if he said 'I'll get over it' – but he did, even moving up and making the pass that gave Hunt his gentle nod for the opening goal. How did Byrne manage to keep that injury hidden from Leeds, a team usually so full of nous? Byrne could have been voted Man of the Match and put up for membership of the Secret Service on the same day. Versatile Geoff Strong was another who had a fine Cup final; he was good value, if not great in any position. Jim Beglin, a similar player to Byrne, had gained medals for the League and Cup Double before he had played fifty senior games, but a broken leg virtually ended his active career soon afterwards. He had succeeded Alan Kennedy, nicknamed 'Barney Rubble' after the cartoon character. Kennedy scored late goals, from deep, in League Cup finals against West Ham and Manchester United, and scored again in a European Cup final, against a Madrid team more artificial than Real. Then, he could have died an even happier man after scoring the deciding penalty in the Euro shoot-out against Roma. But all these heroics, vital though they were (and still are), disguised some defensive deficiencies. So Barney is still only fourth behind Nicol, Lindsay and Byrne. Rob Jones does not figure because he has not lived up to the enormous promise he showed in his early days at Anfield after being plucked from Dario Gradi's academy at Crewe. Jones has not had the best of luck; even so, his progress seems to have slowed. John Scales was a substitute who helped Wimbledon beat Liverpool at Wembley, turned up at Anfield five years later and has gone on to reach the England squad. So has Neil Ruddock, which may indicate the lack of international-class talent available to England. A big man and a big presence, but the Kop usually are more discerning in their bestowal of cult status. Phil Babb looked very good when playing for the Republic of Ireland in the 1994 World Cup: was it perhaps because the slower pace under the American sun suited him? Babb, Scales, Ruddock, Wright and Jones cost over £12m between them. Will any of them eventually qualify for the Best Ever team? I doubt it.

My Liverpool Greats would play a loose 4-4-2, sometimes 4–3–3, sometimes more offensively minded than that. So King Kenny would be a nominal wing-half-cum-winger, covered by Terry McDermott, shuttling around the same pasture. Terry Mac had critics aplenty, but what a heart. What stamina. And, on occasions, what a shot. He was Scouse born and bred, slipped through the Anfield scouting net, but eventually turned up at his natural home via Bury and Newcastle. He and Alan Kennedy, then only nineteen, were among the disunited Newcastle side torn apart by rampant Liverpool in the 1974 FA Cup final, but won many an honour after that to wipe away the memory of the mocking chants aimed at Malcolm Macdonald to an Andrew Lloyd-Webber tune: 'Super-Mac, superstar, how many goals have you scored so far?' Perhaps the abiding memory of McDermott is his near-tearful protest after the 1978 League Cup replay defeat by Nottingham Forest when he had a goal disallowed for handling. 'Hit me on the tit, it did,' he groaned. 'I chested it down and volleyed it in. Never did I handle it.' With that and 1974 and the 1977 FA Cup defeat by Manchester United, Mac's record in the biggest of the big games was not of the best. But his goal against Borussia Mönchengladbach went a long way towards softening the pain.

The Dalglish–McDermott pairing in my team is supplemented by Souness and Ray Kennedy as the other half of the middle four. Souness was absolutely, totally, one hundred per cent fearless on the field, no matter what was going on around him. He could dish it out, but he could take it too, and often enough he was ignoring the rough stuff and getting on with the job of making goals, or scoring them. He was the first Liverpool player to get two hat-tricks in Europe (followed by Saunders and Rush) and averaged a goal every seven games, sharp shooting for a midfielder. As a strong personality, he made a splendid captain, and something disappeared from the midfield when he went to Sampdoria. (What a pity that almost a decade later, in managerial form, he came back to tarnish so much of his well-earned reputation.) Ray Kennedy made a slow start at Anfield, where he had to live down the fact that he had helped Arsenal to beat the Reds in the 1971 FA Cup final. As a striker he looked ponderous and he took a long time to settle, but then Paisley switched him to midfield and a new career began. When it ended, he had at least one medal from five of the six competitions open to English clubs (the Cup Winners' Cup being the exception) and seventeen England caps. Kennedy has gained many more admirers since his retirement, through his courageous struggle against Parkinson's disease, a particularly cruel fate for a man who had such strength and stamina in happier days.

For a time, as the 1970s turned into the 1980s, Liverpool's midfield was perhaps the best club quartet in the world. Three of the four figure in my team, the only discard being Jimmy Case. Somebody had to step aside for Dalglish, but Case would be my first choice for substitute. Why did he never win an England cap . . . or ten? A very talented player indeed, our Jim, and as tough as they come, as he proved by playing on past his fortieth birthday, despite problems with his hearing. He was unfortunate to be on the losing side in two FA Cup finals, for different clubs (Liverpool and Brighton) against the same club, Manchester United. He scored a superb goal in the first, catching a long pass on a thigh, swivelling and shooting all in one movement, and almost collected a consolation goal for poor battered Brighton, managed by another ex-Anfield midfielder, Jimmy Melia, with a shot that bounced off Bailey's bar. Melia had been a useful player over almost a decade, but was one of those who never had the Anfield crowd wholly behind him. He was a touch too tender in the tackle, although good enough to gain two caps before moving on to Wolves and Southampton. I was surprised, when checking the records, to find that Melia had scored as many as seventy-six goals in 269 League games, because he was not generally known as a marksman. An early start helped: he made his debut when only eighteen.

There is plenty of midfield competition, notably from Jason McAteer, of the current crop, Jamie Redknapp and Steve McManaman, and two of the older vintage, Jan Molby and Ronnie Whelan. Molby made an indelible impression, with his physique, his skill, his Scouse accent, and the strength of character he showed when coming back from his jail term for driving offences. Stone walls do not a prison make and big Jan, thrusting his way to the top again after that dreadful experience, demolished many a defensive stone wall with his passing. Whelan, now managing

Southend, was sometimes derided, possibly unfairly, by those with short memories. To me, he always appeared to be a player of considerable value, one-pace but multi-pass, blessed with a gift for scoring goals at vital moments. Three in League Cup finals; strange though it may appear, as I write, nobody has scored more in the competition's thirty-five-year history.

Wingers are now called wide midfielders, and Liverpool have had their share of good honest worker-wingers/wide midfielders. Such as Ian Callaghan. Imagine it: twenty years at Anfield, 848 senior games, thousands of miles spent chasing around ground after ground, and scarcely a foul committed. Towards the end I thought his back would give out through bending to tie so many bootlaces, but even as his fortieth birthday approached he still had the teenager's fresh outlook. He won eleven gongs, including a Second Division championship medal, was on the losing side in four finals in three competitions, was Footballer of the Year in 1974, won a remarkably low four caps over a remarkably long twelve years, and did not have a single enemy. Craig Johnston and Sammy Lee were endowed with Cally's enthusiasm, manifested in their determination to maximise their talents and minimise their faults. One was a tough-minded adventurer from exotic parts (born in South Africa, raised in Australia), the other a butcher's boy with 'Liverpool' running through him like 'Blackpool' through rock. They had their critics, but their good games far outstripped their bad ones. Steve McMahon, another Merseysider, began at Everton and reached Anfield via Aston Villa. A hard case (or in Liverpoolese, 'an 'ard case') who gave his all for his clubs and his country. If more Reds at Wembley in 1988 had followed his example, the dreadful shame inflicted by Wimbledon might have been averted. Ray Houghton was a battler, too, as polite as they come when off the field but a surprisingly tough nut on it. He was Scottish-born and a true patriot in the green of the Irish Republic. Few of the many who have worn those colours have done so with more distinction. Nigel Clough, totally different from Houghton, looked so very, very good when he was at Nottingham Forest, despite his lack of initial pace; at Anfield, the gold turned out to be mere gilt. Stig Bjornebye, bought at a quarter of the cost of Clough, proved a better bargain. Rumour has it that Alex Ferguson saw Stig shoot a wonderful goal to win Norway's FA Cup final for Rosenborg, and Souness signed him in an effort to put one over on his biggest rival. Paul Stewart also scored a Cup final goal, for Spurs in 1991, at a time when his conversion from striker to midfielder looked to be one of Terry Venables's most inventive ideas. Then Stewart went to Anfield and his decline was as remarkable for its totality as it was for its speed.

Who else has figured in midfield for Liverpool in my half-century? There was the elegant Phil Taylor, usually in harness with Bob Paisley; both became manager, with widely different success ratios. Johnny Wheeler from Bolton, one of the 1953 Wembley team confounded by Blackpool's Stanley Matthews. 'Trapper' Twentyman, who became chief scout and found Rush, among others. Two unrelated Campbells, Don and

Bobby. Keith Burkinshaw (one game and I saw it), who followed Shankly as one of Workington's managers, and did rather better with Spurs. Gordon Milne, Shankly's godson and a key man in the mid-1960s team until he was suddenly, inexplicably, sold to Blackpool (later he became a successful manager in that hotbed of enthusiasm, Turkey). Tommy Leishman, a Scot succeeded by another Scot, Willie Stevenson, who won the Scottish Cup with Rangers and the FA Cup with Liverpool, and was outstanding in that 1965 success. Little Brian Hall, whose first goal for the club was timed to perfection: the winner in an FA Cup semi-final against Everton. Peter Cormack, a wiry Scot making a huge impact in his early appearances, an impact that he could rarely match later on. John Wark, another Scot, signed from Ipswich in the hope of replacing Souness. And Michael Thomas, a brave man indeed to join Liverpool after snatching the Championship from them with that last-minute Arsenal decider in 1989; the hard-hearted, I suppose, would say that his many injuries since then is just Anfield taking its revenge. (His superb shot at Wembley in 1992 was some atonement.) More than half a century earlier there had been a trio of Scots: Jimmy McDougall, who as captain of Scotland once collected a bouquet from Mussolini; Jock McNab, later landlord of a celebrated Bootle establishment; and a certain Matt Busby, who could have become coach when he returned from war service in 1945 but preferred to go to Manchester United as manager, even though Old Trafford had been badly damaged by bombs and the contract that had been drawn up at Anfield allowed him the use of a club car 'when one becomes available'.

Which takes us to the forward line, if the modern two-man (sometimes even fewer than that) formation can be afforded such a title. Ian Rush, of course, the finest British-born finisher I have seen. Moderate in the air but supremely decisive with the ball at his feet. As brave as they come, too, and what a worker! In his prime, as the main man up front, he also acted as the first line of defence. No back four could afford to blink when Rush was around. How often did he harry opponents into errors in their own half of the pitch? When he arrived at Anfield from Chester they called him 'Clanky' because of his angular frame, but he would have been a hell of a player if he had never scored a goal. I watched him make his third senior appearance, in the 1981 League Cup final replay against West Ham at Villa Park, and never have I seen a player keener to get on the pitch. Enthusiasm? An infinite amount. Record scorer for Wales, in the FA Cup this century, in FA Cup finals, second only to Geoff Hurst as League Cup total scorer, most goals for Liverpool in total, and in both cups, and in Europe. Only Roger Hunt's League total proved beyond him. Failed there, Rushie, didn't you? Still, what can you expect for £300,000?

Enthusiasm was the key to another favourite at Anfield, David Fairclough, but he was never the player Rush became. Fairclough was the original Supersub, in the days before almost every club had bestowed that title on somebody, and his pace made him an excellent surprise to spring on opponents, until his gathering fame led others to suss him out. You would not put him in your best side, and in this sort of company he would not even get on the bench. But he always brought a touch of exuberance to a game, whether he scored or not. And he often did, never more importantly than late on against St Etienne in 1977. Oddly, for a footballer, he later became a journalist. A real one, not ghosted.

Rush is a one-man attack, but in my team I still have one place to fill, and plenty of contenders. Kevin Keegan, for one. If ever a player made the most of himself, Keegan's the boy. He had spent more than three years swanning around Scunthorpe, frequently watched but without any manager taking a gamble on him. Eventually Shankly did – not without some persuasion – and by the time, six years later, that Keegan left for Germany, he had become the latter-day George Best for star quality and popular appeal, with less talent but more common sense. Much more. Keegan, building a modest frame into a mini Charles Atlas, applied himself to ball skill as well, working like stink to make up for his lack of natural ability. He deserved all his many successes, which included seven medals in those six Anfield years, election as Footballer of the Year in 1976, and an eventual total of sixty-three international caps and twenty-one goals. His departure caused some ill feeling, but he certainly did not deserve the spleen vented by one critic: 'You can't help wishing he would fall off his wallet sometimes, just to see the halo dislodged from his perm.' Even so, Keegan does not get into my team. Nor does Roger Hunt, that most dogged of lost-cause chasers, a fiercely fair competitor (booked twice in the 489 appearances which yielded a club record 285 goals). Hunt was very much Anfield's 'Sir' Roger and failed to get some of the plaudits accorded Jimmy Greaves, idol of the southern media; the comparisons and the criticisms hit him harder than he liked to admit. In his defence, I would point out that when Greaves missed the quarter-final and semi-final of the 1966 World Cup through injury, Geoff Hurst deputised for him: Hunt was the established figure. Both were retained for the final, despite the clamour for Greaves to come back, Hurst to stay and Hunt to go. 'Elf' Ramsey ignored the pressure and infuriated the majority of the capital-based media by giving Greaves the elbow. Hurst's three-way hat-trick (header, right foot, left foot) was the stuff of legends whereas Hunt had an undistinguished match. But he had deserved to keep his place in the pantheon of England heroes and, statistically, he was the most successful of all the eleven, on the losing side only twice in his thirty-four appearances. Merseyside loved Roger in a special way because he was a down-to-earth, one-of-us character who made fans feel that dreams are not always doomed to fail. If he could do it, so could they. On that remarkable evening in April 1972, when an England XI played the Liverpool 1965 Cup final team in Hunt's testimonial match, the gates were shut half an hour before the start with 56,000 inside and many more still trying to wheedle their way through the turnstiles. Rain was tipping down, too, yet the fans refused to keep away. Only one Anfield attendance all season was higher, by a mere 117. 'Unbelievable,' said Roger. 'I thought there would be a big crowd, but this . . .' Other Anfield legends have made more money from benefit matches since then, but none drew a bigger attendance, nor had a greater reception.

So Hunt lines up alongside Keegan in my Second XI, getting in ahead of several worthy challengers. Keegan's frequent foil, the amiable John Toshack, is one. He was excellent in the air and pretty good with the ball at his boots, too, yet lacked something. Despite his superb build he sometimes appeared a touch too timid to be a great striker. Perhaps, to quote a Shankly-ism, 'some players get injured a bit too often for their own good'. That might also apply to Stan Collymore, bought for a mind-boggling fee. Initially he seemed unable to adapt to life at Anfield, even when picking up weekly what some unluckier souls do not pick up annually, but the signs are that he has settled. Even so, Robbie Fowler, local boy making good, looks better value. He made a fine start despite an apparently way-ward outlook on life outside the confines of a football pitch. If he progresses along the lines of his first two seasons, his future should be one of constant success. Few players of his generation have scored so frequently.

Fowler was not signed from another League club, and nor was Steve Heighway, found when playing ama-teur soccer for Skelmersdale. Like others such as Cal-laghan, Case, Lawler, Phil Thompson, Tommy Smith and McManaman, their discovery saved the club a for-tune. Heighway was unusual, university-educated and with interests outside the normal run of player pursuits.

His lightning acceleration faded little over a decade, and if his goals arrived at an average of only one every sixth game, they were often of particular importance. You can win wagers by asking the name of the first Irishman to score in two FA Cup finals: punters usually go for Stapleton or Whiteside, but Heighway beat them to it. Other Liverpool strikers since Toshack and Heighway left the scene have included David Johnson, the first man to score for Everton against Liverpool and for Liverpool against Everton. He got two on his debut for England, against Wales, and another two against Argentina a little later without ever fitting the bill one hundred per cent. Before him there was Ian St John, the Red Monkey to Evertonians, a fine player although a wee bit too wee to be an ideal striker. His temper did not help: he was sent off four times while with Liverpool, twice in friendlies. He preceded his fellow Scot, Hansen, in the graduation from dressing room to TV studio, and is making a pretty good fist of it, too.

Eventually a trio of big-money men arrived and made the £35,000 that Shankly paid for St John look an even better bargain. Peter Beardsley, John Barnes and John Aldridge all had great success and enormous popularity at Anfield, and all gave excellent value for the sums they cost. Beardsley, rabbit-quick and far stronger physically than appearances suggest, was a Dalglish import and a Souness export. He had the last laugh by doing well at Everton, of all places, and doing even better when returning to his native territory and starring for Newcastle. Barnes, wonderfully gifted, is still a very fine player but whenever I watch him (Wembley against Manchester United, for example) I cannot help feeling that he can play much better. He has ample courage, and is not afraid to employ that splendid physique. He has mental courage, too, doing his best to ignore the taunts of those bigots playing the racial card. He has come back despite a string of injuries that would have broken lesser hearts. He has been Footballer of the Year twice. And yet that missing something, whatever it is, has held him back. Aldridge was, still is, a complete contrast. If Barnes has not always used his talents to the full, Aldo has used his to the maximum. Awkward, yes, but always a danger in the penalty area. Look at his scoring record. Few players have done as well. Dean Saunders was one who did not. Very sharp off the mark, and a good finisher, but twenty-four goals in sixty games, nine of them against European no-hopers, was not too distinguished a record, especially for a man who cost nearly £3m in the early 1990s. (Incidentally, Roy and Dean Saunders are the only father-and-son pairing ever to play for Liverpool.)

In the early part of this century, first Sam Raybould and then Jack Parkinson topped the First Division scorers in one season. Both, plus Harry 'Smiler' Chambers and Dick Forshaw, scored over a century of goals for Liverpool. Then, for a decade from 1925, Gordon Hodgson set about defences to such good effect that in 378 games he claimed 240 goals. Although a South African, he qualified for England and gained three caps, as well as playing cricket for Lancashire. He once took all ten wickets in a club match against a team of police-men, and could clout a baseball hard and high (baseball was quite popular on Merseyside in the 1930s). Hodgson's total remained the club record until Hunt took it from him, but Jack Balmer would have bettered everybody if, in a career which lasted from 1935 to 1952, he had enjoyed more of the form he displayed in one golden fortnight in the first post-war season: in two weeks he scored hat-tricks in three successive games – three at home to Portsmouth, four at Derby, three at home to Arsenal – which was not a record, as has been claimed, but was highly unusual and highly spectacular. A fearsome winter descended soon after-wards, which led to the season's extension into June. Eventually the sun returned and Balmer scored a daz-zling goal in a Molineux heatwave, to help beat cham-pions-elect Wolves, and take the title to Anfield. Balmer eventually racked up ninety-nine League goals and twelve in Cup ties but was never a favourite, lacking the heart that should have gone with his skill. Three other survivors from pre-war days, Willie Fagan, Berry Nieuwenhuys and Cyril Done, also gained Champion-ship medals that season. Dalglish reminded me of Fagan by the manner in which he could screen the ball from opponents by using what my father used to call 'the backside body swerve' – in other words, sticking the rump into the tackler's midriff. Fagan, a somewhat pedestrian inside-forward, was one of only two men who played in FA Cup finals before and after the Second World War – Horatio Carter was the other – for Preston in 1937 (as a clubmate of Shankly's) and

Liverpool in 1950. Unlike Carter, who won both, Fagan lost both. South African Nieuwenhuys, known as 'Nivvy', was a lanky, lively right-winger in the days when foreigners were strange beings in English soccer. Big Cyril was largely a reserve but was a strong, brave striker who later did well with Port Vale (I saw him score all Vale's goals in a 4–3 win over Liverpool) and Tranmere.

That 1947 title success also owed much to Albert Stubbins, who arrived from Newcastle and soon became a huge favourite, retaining his popularity during and after a lengthy dispute with the club, when he wanted to return to the north-east to live. Not surprisingly, manager Kay and the board wanted him on closer call than that. The row, and a succession of injuries, took a toll on Stubbins, but he is still revered by many followers from my generation, although we admit that his total of eighty-three goals in 180 senior games should have been far higher. His celebrated headlong dive across the snow to nut a low free-kick beyond Birmingham's Gil Merrick in an FA Cup tie remains perhaps the most remarkable goal I have seen a Red score. The free-kick was hit extremely hard. How a man as big as Stubbins took off from the icy surface and got from the perpendicular to the horizontal in time to meet it remains one of life's many mysteries.

That free-kick was taken by the eleventh man in my eleven, the wonderful Billy Liddell. While admitting to as much bias as the next supporter, I have tried to be objective with my selections, and I acknowledge that

the great players of my youth would have little chance
of succeeding in today's frenetic atmosphere – but that
is assuming the players of my day were still as they
were then. Some had gone through six years of war.
They had known food rationing. They travelled by old-
fashioned trains (even more old-fashioned than today)
or charabancs on the roads that preceded motorways
by decades. They wore thick jerseys and lengthy shorts,
carried half a ton of leather laughingly called a boot
on each foot, and often were knocked dizzy by trying
to head the ancient 'casey' ball that grew heavier and
heavier as it absorbed more and more moisture. Tactics
were rudimentary. So was treatment for injuries: in
those days a cartilage operation could end a career;
now, players are back within weeks. Even in those
conditions, with those handicaps, Billy Liddell was a
great player, and an outstandingly fair one. As a winger
or centre-forward he scored 229 goals in 537 club
matches, many of them when successive Liverpool
teams were fighting either to stay up or go up. He was
tremendously strong and fit, despite being a part-time
player all his career. He could fire bullets from either
foot, and I once saw him score with his head from
outside the penalty area (v. Portsmouth, 6 November
1948). He could tackle, he could pass, and he never
stopped working. Off the field, he was a qualified
accountant, later bursar at Liverpool University, a Justice of the Peace and a regular worker for deprived
young people. He played for Great Britain against the
Rest of Europe in 1947, doing little after pulling a
muscle. Eight years on, though then in the Second

Division, he was still good enough to play when the fixture was repeated. Stanley Matthews was the only other GB survivor. With modern medicine, training, diet, transport and tactics, Liddell and many an old-timer would do all right today. And Liddell for one would be worth modern money. Ironically, his time on the Anfield books ended just as the maximum wage was being removed.

When Liverpool reached the FA Cup final in 1950, losing to Arsenal, Liddell was eleven to Jimmy Payne's seven. Payne had come into the team a couple of seasons earlier after a very brief apprenticeship: a local product with remarkable dribbling skills, and plenty of guts despite a slight frame. No player could continue the form he showed in his first two senior games, against Bolton and Arsenal, when his skill had the crowd entranced. Not until Keegan a quarter of a century later did a Liverpool player make a comparable entrance. Eventually, however, Jimmy lost form and favour, moved to Everton, and was out of the game before he was thirty. For a time, Liverpool had Liddell in the middle, Payne on one wing and Alan Acourt on the other. Acourt was slight but quick, scored some splendid goals, and never gave less than a somewhat limited best. He scored on his debut for England at Wembley and was the injured Tom Finney's deputy in the 1958 World Cup. He was succeeded on the left-wing by Peter Thompson, who made his debut for Preston at seventeen and was only twenty when bought by Liverpool, after scoring a goal that knocked the Reds out of the FA Cup. Thompson, like Payne, sometimes overdid the solo bits, but he was a very entertaining player, chosen in the original forty for two World Cup campaigns. When Shankly used two wingers, Thompson and Callaghan were good enough for Dixie Dean to say, 'If I had played between those two I'd have scored more than sixty goals in a season.' Thompson was sometimes dubbed 'Lord Peter', as Hunt was 'Sir Roger', but Liddell was 'King Billy' – proud of his twenty-eight caps for Scotland, proud of his twin boys, and a lovely, lovely man.

So this is my choice for the All-Time Great Liverpool XI, in 4–4–2 formation

Bruce Grobbelaar

Tommy Smith   Mark Lawrenson   Alan Hansen   Steve Nicol

Kenny Dalglish   Terry McDermott   Graeme Souness   Ray Kennedy

Ian Rush   Billy Liddell

Subs: Ray Clemence   Emlyn Hughes   Jimmy Case

John Barnes   Roger Hunt

Chapter Seven
The ten greatest games

Not all great games end in victory for your favourites. For example, two of the most exciting matches I've seen happened in the space of a week and brought Liverpool only one point. That was in 1972, when they lost by the only goal at Derby, the eventual champions, and then drew 0–0 at Arsenal when only victory could keep their title hopes alive. Two minutes from time John Toshack had a goal disallowed for offside. 'Never, never, never,' squeaked Emlyn Hughes later, tears rolling down his face, but he, like the rest of us, had to be content with third place. And that after the team had won thirteen and drawn one of the previous fourteen fixtures. For sheer unremitting tension, those were two remarkable matches.

Going back a long way, to 1946, I recall a 1–5 home defeat by Wolves, when Denis Westcott, a Merseysider by birth, scored four times and hit a post, all in the first half, at the Kop end. Even though Liverpool took the Championship that season (winning 2–1 at Wolves in their last match) the memory of that humiliation refuses to fade. There have been other shocks that will not die: 0–1 in the Cup at Gateshead, where the fans chanted for the referee to call it off because of fog (as happened at nearby Newcastle); not long afterwards, 1–2 at Southend, followed by the worst of all, 1–2 at non-league Worcester City; and, a long time after, Wimbledon at Wembley. In recent seasons there have been defeats in various knockout contests by Bradford City, Brighton, Bolton, Bristol City and Brøndby, to look at only one letter of the alphabet. Bad times live on as well as good.

When it comes to selecting the really big events, however, human nature tends towards success rather than failure. Choosing the ten greatest games in Liverpool history is hard enough without allowing many wrong 'uns to get in the way. So my eventual mulled-over, revised, revised and again revised selection comprised eight wins and two draws. Without having to think too hard, or to consult any records, the initial list numbered twenty-eight. Not surprising, really: Liverpool have actually *won* sixteen major Cup finals (all in the past thirty-one years) so there were sixteen big ones for starters, let alone any of the matches en route. And this did not take into account a single fixture in the League, where Liverpool's eighteen wins leave them standing alone as the champion of champions. Eventually I chose five League matches, three in the FA Cup and two in the European Champions Cup.

Obviously the recent past dominates any such list but the old-timers deserve a mention, too. In any sport, you can only beat (or lose to) opponents who are around in that period. At various times in the club's first seventy or so years of existence, those who were around were the best then, but my first three chosen matches happened in seasons when the club won nothing. They were, and still are, examples of the freakish results that sometimes happen and add so much to the fascination the game holds. Then I went for perhaps the greatest Liverpool victory of all for anyone lucky enough to see it, in 1965. After that, selection became really hard. Eventually my choice involved six games at Anfield, two at Goodison Park, one in Rome and one at Wembley. Four of the ten were against Everton; although the majority of the meetings between the local rivals have been desperate, scrambling, over-hyped battles of attrition, occasionally there is something way, way out of the ordinary. There certainly was in these four.

Choosing the Big Ten took longer than writing about them, hindsight and historical perspective being such a boon. Please feel free to disagree.

Liverpool 6 Newcastle 5
Division One, 4 December 1909

According to the esteemed Association of Football Statisticians, there had been 141,091 Football League games played up to 1991, and only eight of them had ended with a 6–5 home win. This one was the strangest of the lot, for Liverpool came from three goals down to do so. They were trailing 2–5 at half-time, yet recovered to beat the then outstanding team in England.

In seven seasons, starting in 1904, Newcastle won the Championship three times and were fourth three times. In the same period they reached the FA Cup final five times, but won only once. At the time of this remarkable visit to Merseyside they had twelve internationals on their books (when games against opponents from outside Britain were unknown), and they were the reigning champions. Exactly a year before being turned over at Anfield they had lost 1–9 at home to Sunderland but went on to take the title with seven points to spare.

The United team included Irish international Billy McCracken, known as the Offside King for the manner in which he trapped opposing forwards; the splendidly named Colin Campbell McKechnie Veitch (English, and an international to prove it); and Albert Shepherd, a legendary character who, among other diversions from the norm, walked off the pitch in one match because he was so disgusted with his own performance. Shepherd had no need to reproach himself at Anfield. After Howie headed United into a first-minute lead and Jim Stewart equalised, Big Albie took over. He put two in two minutes past Sam Hardy, not looking very much like England's top goalkeeper on this particular day and, after Jack Parkinson had pulled one back, Shepherd scored twice more before the break.

Legend has it that as the players left the field for half-time, one of the Newcastle team (Shepherd perhaps?) said to Liverpool's Jim Bradley: 'You lot will make a good Second Division outfit', or something similar. Perhaps the insult had an effect: Liverpool were higher than Newcastle in the table at that point (in the end they were second to United's fourth). Perhaps the crowd on Spion Kop made a difference. That huge mound, bereft of both concrete and a roof, had been opened only three years earlier. Many of the 22,000 present were gathered there and Liverpool attacked that goal after the break. Up to that point in history, references to the Kop in the local press had been few. From then on, the place had a reputation as a reviver of struggling Reds. 'Kicking into the Kop in the second half is always worth a goal' is a saying proved true as often as not. Many a heart-stirring rally has been launched to the accompaniment of that enormous roar, echoing back and forth. Whatever the reason, Liverpool were transformed. Early in the second half Parkinson claimed his second goal, on his way to a total of thirty that made him the League's top scorer that season. Not long afterwards Ronald Orr made it 4–5. Orr, a Scottish international, had been signed from Newcastle, who regretted his move all the more when he went on to score the equaliser. And with five minutes left, Liverpool in full cry, and United on their knees, Orr began the move that ended when winger Arthur Goddard headed in the winner.

Another legend says that Liverpool's secretary-manager, Tom Watson, fearing more of the same, had locked himself in his office at half-time rather than watch the second forty-five minutes. Eventually the noise brought him out, just in time to see Goddard's goal. Who knows if it's true? But if it isn't, it should be.

THE TEN GREATEST GAMES

Liverpool: Hardy, Chorlton, Rogers, Robinson, Harrop,
Bradley, Goddard, Stewart, Parkinson, Orr, McDonald.
Newcastle: Lawrence, McCracken, Whitson, Veitch, Low,
McWilliam, Rutherford, Howie, Shepherd, Higgins, Wilson

FOOTNOTE: Later that season Newcastle won the Cup for
the first time – on Merseyside. They beat Barnsley 2–0 at
Goodison Park, with Shepherd scoring twice, after a draw
at Crystal Palace. And in the following season, when Liverpool were beaten 6–1 at Newcastle, Shepherd hit another
four.

Liverpool 7 Everton 4
Division One, 11 February 1933

One of the most remarkable in the long series of Merseyside derby games was watched by a crowd of only
moderate proportions, at least as these hugely attractive
affairs go: 44,000 saw this one, some 17,000 below
the Anfield capacity at that time. Any 7–4 result is
remarkable. According to the Association of Football
Statisticians, there were only eighteen in Football
League fixtures from 1888 to 1991, and Liverpool
figured in three of them – this one, one in 1907 when
they beat Manchester United, and one in 1946 when
Chelsea, six down after an hour, scored four times in
a hurry and even looked like rescuing something until
Liverpool scored a seventh (this match also was remarkable for being the official debut, after wartime service,
of those two Anfield heroes, Bob Paisley and Billy
Liddell).

The country was in Depression in 1933, with soaring

unemployment. A cold, damp day did not help, but the uninspired form of the two clubs so far that season also kept would-be supporters indoors. Liverpool had lost four and drawn four of their fourteen home games, and were out of the FA Cup. Everton had won only twice and drawn once in fifteen away matches, and they had been struggling for goals, the feats of the two preceding seasons drifting into memory. What a period that was to be a Blue – successive Second and then First Division Championships with 121 and 116 goals respectively! Seems unbelievable these days, but it happened.

The great William 'Dixie' Dean was then the Everton king, centre-forward, captain, England international and smasher of scoring records. When he smacked in an early opener at Anfield, with keeper Elisha Scott a little slow to get down to the shot, an Everton win seemed highly likely. But then Harold Barton took over. Barton was a former butcher's boy turned winger or centre-forward of no great class, who did better after leaving Anfield than he did while there. He helped Second Division Sheffield United to get to the Cup final, and was in their promotion-winning side three years later. But Barton scored only twenty-nine goals in 106 senior games for Liverpool. Nothing there to rave about . . . apart from two matches: he hit four in a Cup tie at Chesterfield, and he claimed three in this match, the highest-scoring Mersey derby ever staged.

Barton equalised after Dixie's opener, then helped left-winger Alf Hanson (real name Adolph, but none too keen on that) to make it 2–1, and next supplied the pass that Tom Morrison smashed in for 3–1. So to the interval, or the break-for-lemons-period as old 'uns used to call it. Straight from the restart, Tommy Johnson scored for the Blues. That was the sort of thing he did so well, for Manchester City, for Everton and, briefly, for Liverpool. For England, as well: five games, five goals. (What would a Taylor or a Venables give for a man who could promise that ratio?) It wasn't long before outside-right Harold Taylor had made the score 4–2 and with twenty minutes left Barton slipped through, solo, for Liverpool's fifth. Dean rose above everyone to head a third for Everton, Syd Roberts did the same at the other end, and then Barton raced past a couple of weary defenders to complete his hat-trick. Jimmy Stein replied in the last minute but that did not alter the fact that Everton had been humiliated.

Strange, really. As outlined above, Barton had a middling sort of time at Anfield, Hanson stayed for several years without achieving a great deal, and the other three of the five-man forward line, Taylor, Roberts and David Wright, averaged only seventy games each. In contrast, the Everton team included eight internationals and, four months later, that same eleven who had been on the wrong end of this Anfield hiding went to Wembley and beat Manchester City 3–0 to win the FA Cup.

Liverpool: Scott, Steel, Jackson, Morrison, Bradshaw, McPherson, Taylor, Wright, Barton, Roberts, Hanson
Everton: Sagar, Cook, Cresswell, Britton, White, Thomson, Geldard, Dunn, Dean, Johnson, Stein

Everton 0 Liverpool 4
FA Cup fourth round, 29 January 1955

Everton fifth in the First Division, Liverpool twelfth in the Second. Those were the respective standings in the League tables on the morning of this remarkable FA Cup meeting at Goodison Park. Everton had been promoted from Division Two at the end of the previous season, as runners-up to Leicester, and as they went up, so Liverpool went the other way, having conceded ninety-seven goals. The defence continued to leak in the Second Division and in only two games out of twenty-four before this one had they prevented the opposition from scoring. While Everton had a home record of six wins, four draws and three defeats before the Cup tie, the Reds had been having a terrible time on their travels. They had drawn two and lost the other ten of their twelve away games and despite a good home record, with only one defeat, they seemed sadly adrift in the wilds of Division Two after spending forty-nine successive seasons in the First, then the second longest such run in history.

So if ever a Merseyside derby meeting looked cut and dried, this was it – one bookie was giving 6/1 for a Liverpool win, remarkable odds for a derby match with a tradition of close encounters. In the end, the match *was* a virtual walkover, but not for the bewildered Blues. On a muddy pitch, a Liverpool team playing far better than anyone might have expected put on an outstanding display, with a clear edge in skill and perhaps even in spirit. Not that Everton gave up, at least not until the final stages. It was merely that Liverpool, having one of 'those' days, brushed them aside.

Three men stood out. One, Billy Liddell, emphasised yet again how much he meant to his club. They were not dubbed 'Liddellpool' for nothing. Everton knew all about him, although this was the first meeting of the two clubs for four years, and they had made their plans accordingly, yet 'King Billy' was as full of menace as ever. Although nominally centre-forward, he appeared all along the front line, and he was in the outside-left position when he scored the first goal, after eighteen minutes, rounding Eric Moore and smashing a typical Liddell left-foot shot past goalkeeper Jimmy O'Neill. In the second half, when injury forced Laurie Hughes to limp along the left wing, Liddell dropped back to midfield – and he looked pretty good there, too. The nominal left-half, Geoff Twentyman, switched to the centre of defence when Hughes was hurt, and dealt with Everton's most dangerous forward. Dave Hickson, later to move to Anfield, finished a definite second best to Twentyman, who could have been England class if he had only had more pace. The third of the trio, outside-right Brian Jackson, had one of his best days ever. Jackson was only eighteen when he joined Liverpool from Leyton Orient in 1951 for a fee of £7,000 – quite a big sum for a kid in those days. He was very quick and adept on the ball, but lacked consistency and sometimes appeared rather tentative when taking on big defenders. At Goodison, it all came right for him. Liverpool had a trump card, too, in the supporter who wrote to manager Don Welsh before the match pointing out that Everton were vulnerable to free-kicks in their own half, because of their habit of holding a line across the park, then moving forward together to put opponents offside. Welsh and his players had put in plenty of work in training to take advantage, and it paid off.

With half an hour gone Everton were getting back into the game when they conceded a free-kick about forty yards out. Twentyman lobbed it forward, the Everton defence raced away from their goal . . . and the Liverpool attack ran with them. All except one, John Evans, who had hung back in anticipation. As the others, red and blue alike, rushed past him like the Keystone Kops, Evans ran forward, onside (thanks, ref), and alone in front of O'Neill. The plan nearly came unstuck because Evans failed to control the ball, but as the defenders came hurtling back he eventually squared it, Eric Anderson touched it to his left, and Alan Acourt blasted it in for 2–0. In the second half, Evans had two more chances and took them neatly to double the score. First he pushed the ball in after O'Neill had blocked, but not held, a shot from Anderson. Then he timed his jump perfectly to meet Jackson's cross and nodded in the fourth. That was a good way to atone for the previous round: they beat Lincoln in a replay but Evans had become the first Liverpool player to be sent off since Jim Harley on the day before war broke out in 1939.

Liverpool, who had lost 1–9 at Birmingham a few weeks earlier, were not inspired for long. In the next round they lost 0–2 to Huddersfield at Anfield after sixteen successive FA Cup victories on their own ground dating back to 1938. The last team to win there? Huddersfield.

Everton: O'Neill, Moore, Rankin, Farrell, T E Jones, Lello, Wainwright, Fielding, Hickson, Potts, Eglington
Liverpool: Rudham, Lambert, Moran, Saunders, Hughes, Twentyman, Jackson, Anderson, Liddell, Evans, Acourt

Liverpool 3 Internazionale 1
European Champions Cup semi-final, 4 May 1965

If a fairy godmother told me I could see one match again, exactly as it happened at the time, then this would be the one. With hindsight, it probably appears even better than it was. After thirty years we can now put the competing teams in the proper context of time then and now, and identify that particular, peculiar, special period in the history of the city of Liverpool – and, indeed, in the history of Great Britain.

The match was played at a time when, to me at least, Liverpool touched their peak under Shankly, before getting even better under Paisley. The time was also that of the incredible boom in pop music, led notably by the Beatles but supported by myriad other groups and individuals. Poetry and painting, too, were on the crest of the heaving swell. Perhaps even more remarkably, the Royal Liverpool Philharmonic Orchestra also enjoyed a rise in audience figures: more and more people, taking in a quick one at that amazingly ornate

Victorian pub along the road, went to Hope Street and 'the Philly Hall' to see and hear the musicians known locally as the Band of Hope Street. Liverpool, a much-maligned place – which is not to deny that it deserved and does deserve quite a lot of maligning – suddenly was the 'in place', the place for all to be. As an extreme example, even the TV documentary *Panorama* did a Liverpool special, complete with Welsh commentator waxing all lyrical, like. As an even more extreme example, a journalist I know named Eric Black, London born and bred, gave up his job in the capital and moved to Liverpool, where he knew barely a solitary soul, in order to take part in the mass of life there. 'I'll manage,' he said. He did, too. He and I were together when Liverpool beat Inter on Anfield's greatest night.

The background to this marvellous match needs some explanation. Liverpool had gone into European competition for the first time in seventeen years having won the 1963/4 Championship. Twelve months of their mixture of pace, persistence and passing ('Just give it to a red shirt, son, and you'll do for me' as Shankly said to at least one debutant) had taken them to Wembley for the 1965 FA Cup final where, on a wet afternoon, they had played Leeds off the park in the most one-sided 2–1, extra-time victory anyone had ever seen. Up to then Liverpool had never won the FA Cup. As the years passed, even the diehards began to fear that they never would. Evertonians said that the Liver birds, the mythical creatures atop the Liver Building overlooking the Mersey shore, would fly

before Liverpool won the Cup. Those of comic persuasion (and what Scouser is not?) claimed that a virgin
would cross Lime Street before Liverpool won the
Cup. Yet they did it, after seventy-three years of trying,
and only four days later European champions Inter
Milan came to Anfield for the first leg of the Champions Cup semi-final with a hardened, pragmatic squad
of Italian internationals illuminated by three superb
imports – the Spaniards Suarez and Peiro, and the
Brazilian Jair – all under the iron rule of Helenio Herrera, one of the first foreign coaches whose fame had
spread to insular England.

Inter were indeed a splendid club. In twelve years
from 1955 they won the European Cup and the World
Cup championship twice each and the Italian title three
times. In taking the European title in 1963/4 they
had won six and drawn three of their nine games,
removing Everton en route and beating Real Madrid
3–1 in the final. The following season they had a first-
round bye, then beat Dynamo Bucharest 7–0 on aggregate and Rangers 3–2. Their knowledge of European
matters was much greater than Liverpool's. After an
11–1 stroll through two legs against KR Reykjavik in
their first European venture, Liverpool beat Anderlecht
3–1 and 1–0, but struggled to dispose of Cologne in
a remarkable quarter-final. The game in Germany was
goalless; the second leg was postponed, shortly before
kick-off, because of a snowstorm. A fortnight later it
was played and ended 0–0, thanks to a magnificent
display by Cologne keeper Tonnes Schumacher. In
those pre-shoot-out days a third match was arranged

for Rotterdam, where Liverpool led 2–0, were pulled back to 2–2, then went through when the dual-coloured disc tossed by the referee landed red side down . . . after it had stuck on its edge in the mud at the first spin. Three days later Liverpool beat Chelsea 2–0 in the FA Cup semi-final to set up their meeting with Leeds. On the day after that Wembley game, the team and officials returned to Merseyside for a triumphant drive through streets so densely packed with thousands upon thousands of fans that around 500 needed treatment for crush-related injuries. The next day right-back Chris Lawler got married and spent his wedding night in a Blackpool hotel with his teammates.

On the day of the game Inter – Herrera, Suarez, Peiro, Jair and all – were given the shock of their lives by continuous and deafening noise all around Anfield. Inter must have been aware of it even in the dressing-room. They ran out first and misguidedly went to the Kop goal for the kick-in, not knowing that any team usurping Liverpool's right to occupy that end would be less than welcome. As Inter retreated, chastened, towards the Anfield Road area, the Liverpool team emerged, accompanied by two injured players, Milne and Byrne, carrying the FA Cup on a lap of honour. It was a marvellous sight, unless you were Italian. Within three minutes, the roars grew even louder as Hunt, smashing at a waist-high pass, sent it wide of goalkeeper Sarti for one of the finest of that huge collection of Hunt goals. Inter seemed hesitant and overawed, yet equalised when Yeats, trying to clear with his 'swinger' right foot, botched the job and let Peiro get away to make the cross that Mazzola hit past Lawrence. Mazzola was not renowned as a scorer. Nor was Callaghan, but in the thirty-fourth minute he restored Liverpool's lead with a shot from a narrow angle after a clever free-kick routine involving Stevenson and St John. Another goal soon followed, from Lawler, but it was ruled offside by referee Kainer. It was a controversial decision but at the time it seemed unimportant for Liverpool were so much on top, defying the physical and mental strain of a long season – this was their fifty-eighth competitive match in thirty-seven weeks – that more goals seemed sure to follow in the second half. In the end, there was only one. Inter, presumably roasted at half-time by Herrera, gathered in defence and played for the second leg. Sarti saved from Hunt, from St John, from Lawler, from Hunt again and St John again. Even Yeats went up and forced Sarti into yet another stop. With sixteen minutes to go, the pressure paid off. Sarti could only parry a Hunt shot, and St John scored off the rebound. The Kop adapted the tune of *Santa Lucia* to sing, 'Oh Inter, one-two-three, go back to Italy,' but that vaunted defence, so far stretched as to twang like elastic, nevertheless had kept the margin to two goals by the time Anfield's greatest match was done.

The second leg, eight days later, was grim anti-climax for Liverpool. If it had been played sooner, when the combined euphoria of Wembley 2–1 and Anfield 3–1 had not faded slightly, Liverpool might have become the first British team to figure in the Champions Cup final. As it was, by reaching the semi-final they had gone as far as any other team had done in ten seasons of trying. But the memory of the San Siro still rankles.

Liverpool, based in Cernobbio on Lake Como, had two nights of disturbed 'rest' as hordes of Inter fans travelled the twenty-five miles from Milan and made the night hideous. The team's arrival on the pitch was the signal for a mass explosion of fireworks and smoke bombs, amid noise that made even the Kop seem restrained by comparison. Above all, there was the referee, Ortiz de Mendibil from Spain. Even at a distance of thirty years, with some of the participants in the match now dead, I hesitate to claim that the outcome was arranged in advance. There is no proof. Indeed, de Mendibil served on the Uefa Referees' Committee for a time. But he was believed to have a handicapped child whose treatment was extremely costly. Roger Macdonald, in his book *Britain versus Europe*, wrote that the referee 'had what even neutral observers thought was an extraordinary influence on the game'. Brian Glanville, in *Champions of Europe*, was in no doubt that de Mendibil was wrong to allow not only the first Inter goal, but the second (he also pointed out that this was one of five European matches involving Italian clubs that de Mendibil handled, with this perhaps predictable outcome: Italy 5, The Rest 0).

Liverpool, to a man, were outraged. Shankly even claimed that after the first leg, an Italian visitor to Anfield had told him: 'You will not be allowed to win this tie.' I am positive that de Mendibil signalled an indirect free-kick when Moran committed an early tackle that did not deserve any punishment, let alone a goal, but when Corso shot the ball directly past Lawrence, a goal was given. Then Lawrence was bouncing the ball when Peiro kicked it away from him and shot into the empty net. I doubt if any referee other than de Mendibil would have allowed that. In ten minutes Liverpool had lost the lead so valiantly obtained at Anfield, and from then on they were always chasing the game. Facchetti scored a magnificent third in the second half, finishing an eighty-yard movement, and Liverpool had to wait another eight years before lifting their first European trophy.

Inter, lucky enough to stage the final on their own ground, retained the Champions Cup by beating Benfica, who were reduced to ten men, by scoring the only goal . . . through the keeper's legs. But they admitted they were lucky to be there. As Herrera put it after the first leg: 'We have been beaten before, but never defeated before. Tonight, we were defeated.'

(at Anfield)
Liverpool: Lawrence, Lawler, Moran, Strong, Yeats, Stevenson, Callaghan, Hunt, St John, Smith, Thompson
Internazionale: Sarti, Burgnich, Facchetti, Tagnin, Guarneri, Picchi, Jair, Mazzola, Peiro, Suarez, Corso (Bedin for Tagnin was the only change for the return match)

Borussia Münchengladbach 1 Liverpool 3
European Champions Cup final, 25 May 1977

This victory is remembered as the one that ensured Liverpool's magnificent double of League Championship and Champions Cup in the same season, with a losing FA Cup final sandwiched in between. Often, and incorrectly, it is mentioned as the club's first European trophy, which does an injustice to some earlier players. How easily we forget as time goes on: Liverpool had won the Uefa Cup twice before this, at their first two attempts after the renaming of the old Fairs Cup. In 1973 they beat Borussia, winning 3–0 at home after both sides had missed a penalty and then, somehow, surviving a right shellacking in Germany with no more than a 0–2 defeat. In 1976 they beat Bruges, coming back from 0–2 down at home to win 3–2, then drawing in Belgium.

Unfortunately for Lawler, Lindsay, Lloyd, Cormack, Hall, Boersma and Toshack, who all played in one or both of the Uefa games against BMG, they did not appear in a Champions Cup final. All twelve who played against Bruges later appeared in at least one of the showpieces, which is a roundabout way of trying to prove that Liverpool were growing and refining as time advanced, as Shankly turned to Paisley (and then, later, to Fagan and to Dalglish). By the time 1977 and the second final against Borussia came around, Liverpool were *the* outstanding club of English soccer history. Yet only three of the individuals in action at that time – Smith, Ray Kennedy and McDermott – feature in my Best XI, which shows how many fine exponents of football arts and crafts were to follow them.

A brief spell in May 1977 was perhaps the most momentous of all the hectic periods in Liverpool's history. On 14 May, a 0–0 draw with West Ham at Anfield was enough to clinch the League champion- ship. On 21 May, they lost 1 2 to Manchester United in the FA Cup final despite having most of the play. On 25 May, they played Borussia in Rome's Olympic Stadium. Could they recover from the disappointment of missing the second leg of the domestic double – bad enough in any circumstances, but even worse given that they had been the better side at Wembley? Or would they fail again, in their sixty-first match of an exhausting season? To get to Rome, Liverpool had had to beat Crusaders of Belfast (no problem), Trabzon- spor of Turkey (0–1 away, but three goals in the first fifteen minutes at home), St Etienne of France (0–1 away, then a 3–1 recovery inspired by Fairclough's late arrival as substitute) and FC Zurich (3–1 and 3–0). Confidence was high, but that confidence went through the roof on arrival in Rome. The fans took the place over, a mass invasion of generally good-natured Scousers turning the ancient city into a substitute Kop. The *Liverpool Echo* had printed a splendid souvenir edition which contained myriad information, including the address of the prison, but that was a line of type wasted. This time, thankfully, disturbance was at an absolute minimum, despite the dreadful package jour- neys many of the 30,000 or so fans had faced.

If there was no trouble from the scallies, there was trouble with Cally. A leg injury had been bothering him, and he had hardly played for two months. But Paisley, whose previous visit to Rome had been in a Bren gun carrier during the war, gambled on his prize veteran being able to last the distance. Callaghan did, marvellously well, to take his merited place with the other heroes on a great, great night. The biggest of them all, however, was Keegan. He was on his way out of Anfield after six highly successful seasons, ironically bound for a German club, Hamburg. His decision to go had angered many people, his jaded display at Wembley had upset more. Keegan was as miserable as any after that, and all the more determined to go out on a winning note. Despite facing Berti Vogts, a fine servant of club and country, as his immediate opponent, Keegan achieved his ambition and had a magnificent match.

Off the field, there was no contest. The portable Kop simply drowned out German attempts at an answering chorus, and an increasingly dangerous Red attack had its reward in the twenty-seventh minute when Callaghan set Heighway going on the right, and McDermott hit the final pass wide of Kneib's right hand. That injected rather more urgency into the Germans, but Liverpool were calmly in control until early in the second half, when Case misjudged a back-pass and let an opponent through. As luck would have it, the opponent was the Dane, Allan Simonsen, then approaching his peak as one of the greatest forwards the Bundesliga has known. Simonsen's shot left Clemence helpless, so Keegan and co. had to start all over again.

They did so pretty quickly, thanks to old-timer Tommy Smith. He surprised a statuesque set of defenders, and his own fans, by running forward to meet a corner from Heighway and head it in for his first goal since November 1974. Smith was having a benefit match a few days later and had announced that Rome would be his last competitive appearance. The goal, and the win, persuaded him to add another year. Borussia had had it. Vogts was exhausted. Simonsen had disappeared. So had Heynckes, who had scored twice against Clemence in the Uefa Cup final four years earlier. Only the mighty Stielike looked to be still full of fight. Liverpool, though, needed another goal to be absolutely sure, and with eight minutes to go they got one. Keegan, yet again, scattered the defence with a run, Vogts felled him with a despairing tackle, and Neal put the penalty far out of Kneib's reach. I have seen some Liverpool crowds, but this one topped the lot at that moment. The stadium seemed full to the uppermost edge with red and white.

And so to the celebrations. Paisley, who had been known to pull a cork or two in his time, claimed later that he did not have a drink all night. 'Ah just wanted to savour it all, like,' he said. Others were less restrained. Clemence – who had admitted after the United disaster that he was 'going to get soooooooo pissed' – was a leading celebrant, and a happy journalist went into the pool as a result. McDermott, asked for his autograph by a paperless, penless and almost legless enthusiast, obliged by borrowing a felt-tip and signing the man's underpants. A bunch of fans found the team hotel (a Holiday Inn is not difficult to trace) and joined the players and wives in shifting a giant buffet. Were they invited? Who knows? Only in the cold light of much, much later mornings was a decision made to keep hotel locations secret, to avoid any repetition. The reckoning-up after the party came to 385 bottles of champagne, at a then expensive tenner a go. And why not? Liverpool had gone to a place in football's pantheon where, as far as English clubs were concerned, only Matt Busby's battlers had gone before, and had the Championship trophy as well. What a wonderful feeling it was.

Borussia: Kneib, Vogts, Klinkhammer, Wittkamp, Bonhof, Wohlers (Hannes), Simonsen, Wimmer (Kulik), Stielike, Schaeffer, Heynckes
Liverpool: Clemence, Neal, Jones, Smith, R Kennedy, Hughes, Keegan, Case, Heighway, McDermott, Callaghan

Everton 1 Liverpool 3
FA Cup Final, 11 May 1986

There was no European football for Liverpool in 1985/6, nor for any other English club: all were banned by Uefa as a result of the riot at Heysel Stadium, Brussels, before the Champions Cup final between Liverpool and Juventus. The ban, indefinite at first, was later amended to five years for all English clubs and an extra three for Liverpool, some of whose supporters had been instrumental in the disaster. Eventually the club 'served' a six-year spell without European competition, which had an obvious effect on the balance sheet. In those six years, however, under the management of Kenny Dalglish, Liverpool won the League title three times, were second three times, and

won the FA Cup twice. Players such as Barnes,
Beardsley, Aldridge, Houghton and McMahon were
deprived of the Euro experience, but Liverpool were
still the team to beat. Not many managed it.

Everton looked like doing so for quite a long time
at Wembley in 1986, but eventually were worn down
by a team inspired by Molby and Rush. In February,
Everton had won a League match at Anfield, 2–0.
After that, Liverpool raced away to complete a League
and Cup Double, and they did so by winning fourteen and drawing three of their last seventeen fixtures.
They clinched the first half of the twin objective by
winning at Chelsea in their last League engagement
with a goal by Dalglish, then thirty-five but still full of
running. A week later, however, the Scot was eclipsed
by a Dane and a Welshman. Molby, the Scouse Viking,
rarely could have played better than he did at Wembley.
Twice he almost scored, twice he kept icy calm in a
crowded penalty area before making short but perfectly
timed passes, putting Rush clear to round keeper
Mimms for an equalising goal, then leaving Johnston
with a near-vacant net to hit from six yards. Then
Rush, deep in his own half, joined in a movement
that ended several passes later with Whelan, carefully
sidestepping a drifting blue balloon, crossing for a Liverpool figure on the opposite side of the penalty area
to bring the ball down and smash it past Mimms. The
Liverpool figure? Rush, of course, on the end of a
seventy-yard dash. Watch it on video, and marvel. Rush
might, even should, have had a third goal in the closing
moments, but did not get enough height on an

attempted lob and Mimms, a good deputy for the injured Southall, made the save. Two more goals in 1989 and one in 1992 put Rush clear as the top FA Cup final scorer, but how much nicer figures of 3–2–1 would have been.

Liverpool did well to come back after a dodgy opening in which Lineker, Footballer of the Year in his only season with Everton, caused all sorts of trouble. But he had only one scoring chance, when Reid put him away from Hansen. Mind you, he took it, with his right foot, after Grobbelaar had parried the first effort from his left. Brucie got a hand to the second shot without being able to divert it far enough. No blame for him, and a ton of credit to him in the second half when Hansen's miscued clearance turned into a perfect centre for Sharp. Grobbelaar was well wide of his goal, having gone over in expectation of a back-pass from Hansen, but somehow he got across and, a genuine acrobat, got up as well, to flick the ball over the bar. Everton, unlucky to be deprived of a European place on Heysel grounds after winning the Championship in 1985, were perhaps unlucky to lose by a two-goal margin. They played a full part in an absorbing match, only to incur cruel penalties for giving the ball away. All three Liverpool goals came from moves built up after an Everton man had lost possession. All three errors happened a long way out, and against lesser opposition the effects would not have been so severe. On this day, however, Liverpool were quick and accurate enough to exact full retribution.

It was Liverpool's fifty-seventh match of the season,

and their thirty-seventh victory to set against a mere seven defeats. Some record. And this was the club's second final against Everton, following the Milk Cup derby in 1984. Liverpool won the replay 1–0 after a goalless draw. Then, in 1989, there was a third 'Liverton' clash at Wembley with Liverpool, ahead in virtually their first attack, eventually winning 3–2 in extra time after Stuart McCall had equalised in the last of the ninety minutes. Ironically Liverpool have lost three FA Cup finals after beating Everton in all three of the semi-finals, but they certainly have the edge when meeting their neighbours/rivals on the biggest stage of all.

Dalglish and his men won generous and deserved praise for their Double, with few caring to recall that only an uncharacteristic display had cost the team their chance of a third trophy that season. They got to the semi-final of the Milk Cup, beating Manchester United on the way thanks to two goals by Molby, but then lost to Queens Park Rangers. A 1–0 defeat in the first leg was by no means beyond overturning, but at Anfield Molby missed a penalty and own goals by Whelan and Gillespie enabled Rangers, including former Liverpool forward Michael Robinson, to draw 2–2 and go through on aggregate. Oxford played supremely well in the final by the standards of a team finishing eighteenth in the League beating QPR 3–0, but surely they could not have withstood a Liverpool outfit in full cry. Mind you, we said that before Wimbledon ruined a Double dream in 1988 . . .

Everton: Mimms, Stevens (Heath), Van den Hauwe, Ratcliffe, Mountfield, Reid, Steven, Lineker, Sharp, Bracewell, Sheedy.
Liverpool: Grobbelaar, Lawrenson, Beglin, Nicol, Whelan, Hansen, Dalglish, Johnston, Rush, Molby, MacDonald

Liverpool 5 Nottingham Forest 0
First Division, 13 April 1988

This was the night when it all came right. Tom Finney, the former Preston and England winger, was widely quoted when he called it 'the finest exhibition I've ever seen' but that is only a truncated version of what he said.

Finney played some 700 senior games, seventy-six of them for his country, in a lengthy career. Few people can know football as he does. He is generally sparing with his praise, so he must have seen something out of the ordinary when he said: 'I haven't watched a better display in all the time I've been playing and watching the game. It was absolutely tremendous. You could not see it bettered anywhere. Not even in Brazil – not at that pace. The moves Liverpool put together were out of this world.' Even Kenny Dalglish, another soccer expert not renowned for lavish use of the English language, dubbed this 'an absolutely magnificent display'. The media went potty, as they so often do, and clips were shown over and over again on television for the next few days. That in itself is by no means unusual, but this time what might have been merely the usual overkill was pretty much justified. Liverpool had been turning on the top-quality tap all season. The arrival of John Barnes from Watford and Peter Beardsley from Newcastle during the summer made up, as well as any two players could, for the loss of Dalglish, who was now concentrating almost solely on management rather than player-management, and Ian Rush, who had gone to Juventus for £3.2m (with, fortunately, a buy-back clause deep in the transfer documents). Ray Houghton from Oxford was soon to join Ronnie Whelan and Steve McMahon in midfield; Steve Nicol was fixed at what used to be left-back, although he scored six goals in the first six matches; and Gary Gillespie was having one of his longest spells free from the injuries that dogged him so relentlessly. There was every reason for skipper Alan Hansen to look forward to collecting some more silver come May.

'Jocky' did, but only one trophy. In a season that began with three successive away games, Anfield having been put out of commission because of a sewer collapse at the Kop, Liverpool played fifty matches, scored ninety-nine goals, conceded only twenty-eight and lost a mere four times. The team played well enough to get two or maybe even all three 'pots' available, in yet another year without European games, but they had to be satisfied with the League Championship and a nine-point margin over Manchester United.

The first twenty-nine games of the forty-match League programme produced twenty-two wins and seven draws, equalling Leeds United's record unbeaten run from the start of any season. Match number thirty was at Everton where a single goal gave the Blues their second win over their rivals: they had won 1–0 at Anfield in the Littlewoods Cup four months earlier. The fixtures in the next month were all highly significant. First, a 2–1 win over Wimbledon, whom Liverpool would meet again later that season, at Wembley; then the second League defeat, 2–1 to Forest in Nottingham. Two days later, on Easter Monday, a pulsating battle with Manchester United ended all square at 3–3 and led to United manager Alex Ferguson's outburst about 'clubs leaving Anfield choking back the vomit, knowing they have been done by the referee'. (Pleasing sentiments, charmingly expressed.) On the following Saturday, Forest again, this time in an FA Cup semifinal that Liverpool won 2–1 with the aid of two goals by Aldridge: a marvellous volley after Barnes had made the chance, and a penalty. On the Wednesday, Forest were the opponents for the third time in eleven days. The teams were virtually unchanged. The two other encounters had been hard, fast and cleanly contested. If Liverpool were a little unlucky on Trentside, they had most of the breaks in the Cup tie. In the third game, they dismissed any possible 'lucky' accusations, and reached sublime heights.

Liverpool have had more accurate move-constructors than Houghton. They have had more precise finishers. They have had midfielders with even stronger legs and lungs. But very, very few have combined all those attributes. Houghton revealed all these talents with the first goal, intercepting a pass, bursting away, laying off to Beardsley and then providing a crisp finish. Beardsley did something similar to create the second goal, a delightful chipped shot from Aldridge. Beardsley hit the bar before Houghton crossed for Gillespie, unusually far forward, to make it 3–0. Barnes, beating three men in the space of a few yards, one with the cheekiest of nutmegs, laid on the fourth for Beardsley. And Spackman was involved twice in as many seconds when a breathtaking move left Aldridge clear to take his total of goals against Forest to four in four days. Spackman? An easily forgotten southerner taken north by Dalglish from Chelsea and, on his day, a very useful midfielder. This was one of his days. The Liverpool team left the pitch to an ovation that really justified 'thunderous' as a description, and after that they eased through their final six League fixtures, drawing four and winning two – by a Beardsley goal at home to Spurs that clinched the title, and 5–1 away to Sheffield Wednesday the Saturday before Wembley. There, Wimbledon were waiting. Snarling, sleeves-up Wimbledon, who played out of their collective skins and had the strength of character, plus a fair portion of skill, to end Liverpool hopes of a second League and Cup Double in three seasons. So Liverpool were robbed when Beardsley's early goal was disallowed because the referee had blown for a free-kick, in Beardsley's favour. So Beasant somehow saved from Barnes and from Barnes again, off the rebound, both from a few yards out. So Aldridge, rarely, failed with a penalty (did Beasant move before the kick?). For all that, Liverpool should have won. Dalglish's selection was exactly the same as that which crushed Forest, right down to the two substitutes. What a shame that the thirteen could not retain more than a vestige of that night's magic. The fourth of the season's four defeats spoiled what had been thirty-six weeks of almost total magnificence.

Liverpool: Grobbelaar, Gillespie, Ablett, Nicol, Spackman, Hansen, Beardsley, Aldridge, Houghton (Johnston), Barnes, McMahon (Molby)
Nottingham Forest: Sutton, Chettle, Pearce, Walker (Wassell), Foster, Wilson, Crosby, Webb, Clough, Glover, Rice

Liverpool 9 Crystal Palace 0
First Division, 12 September 1989

Facts foremost. This was Liverpool's record victory in the First Division, and equalled the club's biggest winning margin in any League match (10–1 against Rotherham Town in Division Two back in 1896). Only in the Littlewoods Cup (10–0 v. Fulham, 1986) and Europe (10–0 v. Dundalk, 1969; 11–0 v. Stromsgodset Drammen, 1974) had a nine-goal margin been bettered. The score also was the biggest in the Football League's top section since Boxing Day 1963 when Fulham beat Ipswich 10–1, and the fact that eight players scored for one team was a League first, although not an Anfield first: nine men had done so against Stromsgodset.

Before the off there seemed no reason why this figure should turn into such a statto's delight. Liverpool had begun the season with a win, two draws and another win, scoring seven goals and conceding two.

The squad's composition was much as before, with Ronnie Whelan back after a lengthy absence through injury, and Glenn Hysen, a strong but slowing Swede signed from Fiorentina, and David Burrows, from West Bromwich, the only newcomers. Dalglish was still in charge and the backroom (or bootroom) personnel were still in place. The visitors to Anfield on a mild Tuesday evening in early autumn were Crystal Palace, who had gained promotion at the end of the previous season, after eight years in the Second Division, by recovering from a two-goal deficit against Blackburn in the play-offs. Under manager Steve Coppell, born and raised in Liverpool and a former student at Liverpool University, Palace had begun their latest spell of First Division life by taking four points from four games. They were not fancied to win at Anfield, but nobody could have expected them to be the victims of such a hammering.

Before the game – it was never a match – got going, the forecast was that John Aldridge, one of the subs, would get on at some stage, to make his farewell appearance. Aldridge was due to sign for Real Sociedad, ending a shortish but very successful stay with his hometown club. Since his move from Oxford to Anfield in 1986 he had scored sixty goals in eighty-six matches plus fourteen as sub, including one run of ten scoring appearances in a row and another of eight. He had been an excellent successor to his lookalike, Rush, after the Juventus deal, but Rush had returned, had recovered from a hesitant start, and had won the Cup for his club by repeating the two goals he scored at

Wembley in 1986 with two more against the same opponents, Everton, in 1989. Rush and Aldridge were perhaps too similar to be an ideal combination (although the club certainly did well enough when they were together) and the chance of a big-money move finally persuaded Aldridge that his days as an Anfield hero were nearly done. There was one last moment to savour. The game was won, the score was 5–0, a penalty was awarded and the crowd chanted for Aldridge, who had built up a 'dead-eye' reputation from the spot despite his Wembley miss against Wimbledon. Dalglish sent him on and he promptly hit the ball past goalkeeper Suckling, scoring his last goal for his club with his first kick of his last match. When it was over, Aldridge slung his boots into the Kop where he had stood to cheer the Reds in his younger days.

Nicol, McMahon and Rush had scored in the first half, and Gillespie and Beardsley did so before the penalty. In the last ten minutes Barnes added a seventh, Hysen an eighth, and Nicol rounded off the rout as he had begun it, scoring the ninth. So four of the goals came from so-called defenders on a night when Coppell said: 'We'll remember this to the day we die. My lads came off looking shell-shocked and they had every right to be that way.' Liverpool's overall display, a combination of individual excellence and combined power, carried out at great speed, was reminiscent of that against Forest eighteen months earlier, although Palace were not as good a team. At times Suckling seemed to stand alone against the tide, and though he might have been at fault with two of the goals, he prevented plenty more.

Despite some inconsistencies Liverpool went on to win the title. Not long after the Palace rout there was a run of four defeats in five games, one of them by the only goal against Arsenal at Highbury in the Little-woods Cup. There was a 5–1 win at Chelsea and an 8–0 demolition of Swansea in the FA Cup third round, but by the time Coventry were defeated 6–1 at High-field Road in the final game of the season, dreams of Wembley had evaporated ... because of Palace. The draw paired the clubs in the FA Cup semi-final at Villa Park. Liverpool, not surprisingly, were odds-on to succeed and go to Wembley for a third successive season. In addition to the 9–0 affair, they had won 2–0 in the return League match at Selhurst Park, and Palace were too near the bottom of the table for comfort. Ten of Liverpool's starting line-up had taken part in the Anfield romp: six of the Palace eleven were still trying to erase the memory. Yet the Dalglish defenders picked this of all days to have a mutual stinker, particu-larly at set pieces. Despite a first goal brilliantly taken by Rush, despite a tremendous shot by McMahon, despite a Barnes penalty, Liverpool still did not score often enough. Palace, somehow, nicked four goals in about fifty minutes, three from around six yards out, the last of them in extra time, and went through to Wembley.

Liverpool could hardly be blamed for relaxing when in front at the interval. After two and a half games against Palace they were 12–0 up and once again they were looking well in control. Then the match turned in the space of a few seconds after the restart. McMahon gave the ball away, Pemberton made a long run and cross, a shot was blocked and Bright scored with a superb volley from near waist height. It was a remarkable effort, and it inspired Palace to go on and lead, then do it all again after falling behind for a second time.

So in the end, a rather bitter end, Liverpool had to make do with 'just' one trophy, and missing another final was a bad blow, especially as meeting Manchester United would have given the team a chance to gain revenge for the unlucky defeat that Paisley's 1977 Treble-hunters suffered against those same rivals. Dalglish, apparently, was speechless after the final whistle at Villa Park, and had to go for a shower before he could take part in the first of more than one inquest. I suppose that he, like the rest of us in the immediate aftermath of a remarkable defeat, had forgotten the glory of that 9–0 victory on that September evening. Only later did the memory of it come back . . .

Perhaps the last words on that 9–0 affair should come from Hysen, who had helped IK Gothenburg to win the Uefa Cup in 1987: 'I thought we had a good team there,' he said. 'I played against some other good sides when I was in Italy – Milan, Juve, Inter, Napoli. But Liverpool in this game were on a different planet. I would back them to win against any club, anywhere.' Sadly, not at Villa Park.

The teams in the 9–0 game were:

Liverpool: Grobbelaar, Hysen, Burrows, Nicol, Whelan, Hansen, Beardsley (Aldridge), Gillespie, Rush, Barnes, McMahon (Molby)
Crystal Palace: Suckling, Pemberton, Burke, Gray, Hopkins, O'Reilly, McGoldrick, Thomas, Bright, Wright, Barber

Everton 4 Liverpool 4
FA Cup fifth round replay, 20 February 1991

In half a century of following Liverpool I cannot recall a more remarkable period than the one around this magnificently exciting match, which had my middle-aged heart pumping like a teenager's.

This draw between the Mersey neighbours, which has gone into folklore as the greatest in the long line of derby games, was preceded by Liverpool's 1–1 draw against those other traditional rivals, Manchester United, at Old Trafford, and a 3–1 win over Everton in a League match at Anfield. It led up to a 0–0 FA Cup stalemate on the same ground, and then the truly amazing reply at Goodison, in which Liverpool led four times and still failed to win. Kenny Dalglish's resignation as Liverpool manager followed two days later, with Ronnie Moran's elevation to caretaker. Then came a 1–3 League defeat at Luton, exit from the FA Cup in the second replay against Everton, and a 0–1 Anfield loss to Arsenal, the eventual champions. In between all that there was the retirement of Alan Hansen, whose troublesome knees had failed him for the last time. Moran went on to complete ten games in charge – five defeats, a draw and four wins, including

7–1 at Derby, the club's highest away score this century, and 5–4 at Leeds, where Barnes and his colleagues were four up in half an hour. Then new manager Souness arrived from Rangers, with the title all but out of reach, and the real problems started to pile up. With hindsight, the board might have done better to leave Moran in the post, making use of his forty years of Anfield experience in various capacities, rather than to entrust the job to a former great player, addicted to spending enormous sums on players too often found to be worth far less.

All that, of course, was in the future when Dalglish took his men to Goodison for the Cup replay, after a rather tepid first meeting – as derby games go – at Anfield. Liverpool then had to play without David Speedie, the abrasive Scot recently signed from Chelsea, who had scored against Manchester United and did so twice against Everton in the League a week later, and neither side had revealed much that approximated to top form. A look at the composition of the teams quickly justified Liverpool's position as favourites to win. This was not the finest vintage from the Anfield vineyard, but they had begun the season with a run of twelve unbeaten games and at the time of the first meeting they were top of the table, although they had needed replays to get through their first two knockout rounds. A last-minute own goal earned them a draw at Blackburn, and they were then held 2–2 at home by Brighton. Everton, still relying heavily on their Welsh defenders, Southall and Ratcliffe, were twelfth in the table and had struggled to beat non-league Woking by a single goal in the previous round. If Woking had not given up home ground advantage and agreed to play at Goodison in return for the extra gate money, who knows what might have happened? (Not long after that, Woking decided to copy the 'This is Anfield' sign above the entrance to the pitch at their ground in Surrey, and ordered one saying 'This is Kingfield'. Unfortunately it arrived reading 'This is Kingfiled'.) There were the usual high hopes that precede a derby match but nobody could have expected two such inconsistent groups of players to put on such a thriller, one that was virtually beyond comparison, certainly in my experience. Not for the level of skill involved – there were some awful howlers – but for the remarkably dramatic way in which the game developed.

There were near misses at both ends before the thirty-seventh minute when Rush, the record scorer in Merseyside derby matches, almost added to his total by robbing Watson, racing on and shooting past Southall. Hinchcliffe blocked the ball on the line, but Beardsley lashed it back in. Liverpool one up, and so the score stayed until two minutes into the second half. Then Hinchcliffe hit one of the deep crosses that were to become his trademark, and Sharp's downward header was too strong for Grobbelaar to hold, even though he got both hands to it. Twenty minutes of constant excitement passed before another goal presaged a final twenty minutes of even greater drama. The goal was a magnificent solo effort by Beardsley, who was put in possession by Venison, made ground, and struck a left-foot shot from way out that was perfectly placed beyond Southall's dive. Two minutes later Everton responded again when Nicol, usually so assured on the ball, made a mess of a back-pass that missed Grobbelaar instead of finding him, and was virtually over the line before Sharp helped it in over the last few inches. In twenty-eight previous appearances against Liverpool, Sharp had scored only four goals, one of them a penalty. Now he had added two more in the space of a helter-skelter half-hour.

Only four more minutes had passed when Rush, on Dixie Dean's old Goodison patch, scored a goal that the maestro could not have bettered, rising and heading past the keeper from Molby's cross. Rush's record as a lucky mascot still carried great weight: when he scored Liverpool rarely, if ever, lost, or even drew. So Liverpool fans could hardly be blamed if they did a collective Roy Orbison, thinking *It's Over.* They were in front once more, only thirteen minutes were left, and they had sufficient midfield power to have remained there. Venison takes much of the credit for that, having one of the best games of his mixed time with the club. He had captained Sunderland in a Wembley final when only twenty, and was a useful bits-and-pieces sort of player whose versatility made him a nearly ideal substitute but rarely kept him a regular place for long. After leaving Liverpool for Newcastle he hit some good form and got into the England team, briefly, then signed for Souness, who had taken over at Galatasaray in Turkey. Venison was soon back in England, displaying his curious clothes to the fans at Southampton, and reinforcing the view that he should have made more of his obvious talents. He was one of a posse of red shirts who held out against desperate Everton attacks as time ebbed away. Then, with only seconds to go, Mr Persistent, Hinchcliffe, forced a ball past or even through the lot of them, and substitute Cottee equalised with virtually his first kick.

Amid the eruptions that greeted this life-saver, I felt that Everton might just swing the game their way in extra time. They were lifted by coming back off the ropes yet again, whereas Liverpool were frustrated at having wasted the advantage once more. With half-time of the extra period approaching, however, Barnes conjured up the sort of goal that made him a man apart on days (and nights) when things went well. He swayed between two defenders, then another two, and from the corner of the penalty area he chipped a precise shot clear of Southall's leap. *Still* Everton refused to succumb. Hinchcliffe again got the ball into the area, the defence again failed to get it away, and Cottee scored from close range. Six minutes remained to be contested by twenty-two punchdrunk players and 40,000 punchdrunk spectators, until the final blast on the whistle. The video was on sale within a week. 'Has there ever been a more exciting match?' asked Beardsley. 'There's only one word for it – unbeliev-able,' said Molby. 'You won't see another like that, ever,' said Grobbelaar. Even Dalglish, not one to share his innermost thoughts, seemed unusually lacking in his normal reticence, and enthused about the excitement.

The second replay, a week later, was an anti-climax, not surprisingly. Watson, against his old club, got the only goal, which somehow seemed destined to happen. With Dalglish having retreated from the sound of the guns, Liverpool seemed too drained to raise themselves for another battle. It was the twentieth meeting of the clubs in the FA Cup, a record for the competition, and Everton's sixth win to set against nine defeats and five draws. No matter how often they meet in future, they could never stage a match like this incredible 4–4 battle.

Everton: Southall, Atteveld (McCall), Ratcliffe, Watson, Keown, Nevin (Cottee), Ebbrell, Hinchcliffe, McDonald, Sharp, Newell
Liverpool: Grobbelaar, Hysen, Nicol, Ablett, Burrows, Staunton, Molby, Venison, Barnes, Beardsley, Rush

Liverpool 3 Manchester United 3
Premiership, 4 January 1994

Unlike the theatre, where afternoon performances tend to lack atmosphere, I still believe that soccer is best on the traditional Saturday, with nearly every game starting at three o'clock. No doubt plenty of people feel the same way, but those are the people whose views are less and less important nowadays. Television is the king of soccer, and club marketing managers are the princes. Before many more years have passed, I believe, the majority of games will be on days (or evenings) other than Saturdays, as old habits change and TV's grip becomes ever stronger. I do however admit that there is something about an evening match that heightens the drama for those actually present, as well as for those in their chairs at home, ears assailed by repetitive hype, sometimes over-enthusiastic commentary and seemingly endless analyses. Perhaps it is the flickering shadows, or the way the noises seem to be intensified by the darkness. Perhaps it is because for a brief time you are free from midweek routine. Or maybe it's because night games have a sense of occasion all their own.

In pre-floodlight days plenty of matches were played starting around six p.m, to take advantage of the daylight in spring and late summer. I do not recall seeing many real thrillers then. The same with midweek afternoon games at the same parts of the year: they simply did not compare, for vibrant life and excitement, with Saturdays. Liverpool have played more matches than most clubs, because their successes of the past thirty years have brought a vast expansion of fixtures. Not all the night games have been memorable, of course, but a lot have, and few made greater impact than the clash with Manchester United during the last month of the troubled Souness period.

Liverpool and Manchester have been rival cities for a couple of centuries. That rivalry naturally spread to the football clubs and it has heightened as the years have passed. Unlike the atmosphere for Merseyside derby matches, which are usually played in an excellent spirit despite the pressure of the occasion, meetings between Liverpool and Manchester United are frequently ill-tempered on the field and conducted in an alarming atmosphere off it. Although I believe that football should be open to all wherever possible, and regret the reduction of space for visitors generated by the Taylor Report, I have to admit that there is no longer a case for 'everybody welcome' to apply when United go to Anfield, or when Liverpool visit Old Trafford. The tension leads to a poisonous air of hatred between the rival fans that is genuinely alarming.

All the more reason, then, for this particular meeting to be remembered so warmly. It was played in the frenetic atmosphere that always accompanies such games, but it also showed the Anfield crowd at their finest. Their encouragement for the team hardly slackened, even when United were three goals up inside half an hour. As a Liverpool rally began, and continued, so the crowd maintained a constant roar of support. The fans knew that, as Liverpool teams of the modern era go, this was not a very good one. They knew that Anfield was a place of turmoil as arguments about the manager raged back and forth. They knew that, very largely because of the crowd disasters in Brussels and Sheffield involving themselves and others like them, the traditional Kop had only a few weeks left before the all-seater edict began to be carried out. Every way a Red turned, an era was ending.

And yet, in one convulsive spasm, as if desperate to have one final fling, the fans again earned all the praise that had piled up on those who had gone before. 'The greatest supporters in the world' was Shankly's view of the Anfield brigade (I can hear those 'rrrrs' rolling, even now) and they proved him right again. It was one hell of a game; according to Ruddock, one of many heroes on the night, it was the best he's ever played in. United, from the start, were magical. The directors had barely got their cigars going before Steve Bruce had headed a free-kick past a statuesque defence and wide of Grobbelaar. After twenty minutes Ryan Giggs, one of the finest British talents to emerge for a decade, chipped a second from an angle far too tight for your average performer. Four minutes later, Denis Irwin, a durable full-back with an eye for goal, battered a free-kick just under the bar for the third. United, who had lost only one of twenty-four Premiership matches up to that point of the season, were looking what they were: champions, and on the way to being champions again. And yet the crowd did not give up hope. Their pride was hurt, badly – few teams lead 3–0 at Anfield unless they are wearing red – and there had been little threat from their own team. Yet within moments of Irwin's goal, Nigel Clough suddenly unleashed a low shot from way out that beat an unsighted Schmeichel. The Anfield roar was reborn, the noise coming and coming, crashing and bouncing around the ground. No team could fail to respond and when Clough picked his way between a couple of opponents and unleashed a shot similar to his first, Schmeichel was beaten again.

In the second half, playing towards the Annie Road end, Liverpool dominated. United, a very, very good United, defended resolutely, as they had to. The Koppites, who claim that they can take a collective breath and draw the ball into the goal in front of them, now breathed out as one, in an effort to blow the ball to the other net. And eventually they succeeded, after forty minutes of non-stop action since Clough's second goal, and when only ten minutes remained. Ruddock jumped higher than the rest to reach a cross from Bjorneybye, and his header flew in for the equaliser. Cantona wasted a final United chance – something he did not do at Wembley two years later – and at the last whistle the players fell into mutual embraces involving friend and foe. It was that sort of match – a wonderful, uplifting affair that would restore anybody's faith in the game and its exponents. And its pay-at-the-gate followers.

Liverpool: James, Jones, Dicks, Wright, Ruddock, Redknapp, Clough, McManaman, Barnes (Bjornebye), Rush, Fowler

Manchester United: Schmeichel, Parker, Irwin, Bruce, Pallister, Kanchelskis, Ince, McClair, Keane, Cantona, Giggs

Chapter Eight

Liverpool now, and to come

As the end of the century draws closer, Liverpool are well placed to maintain their position among the leading clubs in Britain. They need to, because their expenditure is enormous, and the manager and his directors and the fans simply cannot afford to wait for a clutch of youngsters to come through if they are to keep in the forefront of the chase for honours: they have to have the finished product. The vicious circle grows ever more vicious, and has done since the advent of the Premiership elevated money to an even higher plane than it was before. A major trophy means bonuses and wage increases for the staff. That increases the amount of revenue needed, so money often has to be spent on new players in the hope of winning more honours, which in turn leads to greater expenditure.

In the past, a mixture of judicious signings, not all of them for huge fees, and home-grown products had been enough to take Liverpool to their unprecedented number of trophies. Fortunately the club now have three young players who, hopefully, will combine with the big-money captures and form the nucleus of assaults on various titles for some years to come. First, in alphabetical order, is Robbie Fowler, a striker of outstanding talent, voted the PFA Young Player of the Year in 1995 and still only twenty-one; yet already well experienced in the ways of the senior football world. Fowler is not the most powerful of forwards, but he has a lot of strength to ride the tackles, and has the born scorer's gift of being able to drift into unlikely looking places, to pick up rebounds or deflections. Playing alongside such a great opportunist as Ian Rush has helped enormously, as he is quick to acknowledge ('If you can't learn from him you need shooting,' he says) although he lacks the Rush instinct for tackling back. Sheer natural talent in and around the eighteen-yard box is his greatest attribute.

He supported Everton when he was a child, then joined Liverpool at fifteen, after scoring eighteen goals out of twenty-three in one junior league match, and represented England at youth level before making his senior debut in a League Cup tie at Fulham in September 1993, when only eighteen. He scored in a 3–1 win, and a fortnight later he claimed all five goals in the second leg. This equalled the club's individual record for one game, set by Andy McGuigan in 1902 (he scored only fourteen times for the club in all) and later equalled by John Evans in 1954 and Ian Rush in 1983. Ironically, Fowler's remarkable performance was seen by only 12,541 spectators. His later scoring feats included the last goal in a local derby match before a standing Kop, in March 1994, his celebrated four-minute hat-trick against Arsenal in the following

August, and a last-minute winner in the home leg of the League Cup semi-final against Crystal Palace in February 1995, followed by the only goal of the second leg. These goals took Liverpool back to Wembley for their first trophy under Roy Evans, the 2–1 win over Bolton, who conceded four to Fowler at Anfield the following September. Fowler was once asked, 'What does it feel like when you get a goal?' – the sort of inanity that footballers have to put up with these days. He gave the questioner a hard stare and answered: 'It's the best feeling there is.' Spoken like a true scorer, a scorer whose sharpness was rewarded with a full international cap, albeit as a substitute, when England played Bulgaria in a friendly at Wembley on 27 May 1996; the first of many, we presume.

Steve McManaman, twenty-four at the time of writing, already is an England international and should be good for many more caps, particularly if he can add more consistency to his game. He is unusually tall for a player who occupies the role that used to be known as winger; now he is employed in a sort of wandering flanker/midfield job, allowed to take himself where he reckons he can be of most use. His close control is something out of the ordinary, and he can do it on the run as well as mesmerising opponents at close quarters. After the 7–0 FA Cup win against Rochdale in January 1996 McManaman was the object of a heart-felt tribute from a breathless defender, the improbably named Dean Martin. 'McManaman,' said Martin, 'runs faster with the ball than most of us run without it.' He does, too, and he doesn't often lose control of it. Apart from having Dean Martin singing his praises, McManaman had come in for some applause from the then England coach, Terry Venables, after his first three appearances in a full international, all as a substitute. They were against an odd assortment of foes, Nigeria, Uruguay and Japan, but no matter whether the opponent was Okechukwu, Aguirregaray or Hashiratani, McManaman showed plenty of potential.

He had played for England under-21s when still eighteen, in December 1990 – a fortnight before making his senior debut for his club – and he collected an FA Cup medal for the victory over Sunderland when he was only twenty. Like Fowler, he was 'a bit of a Blue' as a kid, but gradually changed colour, helped by spending part of his formative years watching players such as Dalglish, Whelan, Molby and Rush. Eventually he went on to help Liverpool to their record fifth victory in League Cup finals, and to help Rush to a record individual fifth winner's medal. Bolton had knocked Liverpool out of the FA Cup in 1993, in a replay at Anfield against a home team lacking both Rush and McManaman through injury. This time, 'Macca' enabled his club to exact revenge, scoring two brilliant goals with individual runs and decisive finishing. Sir Stanley Matthews was the guest of honour on a day the Liverpool lad invoked comparison with that afternoon in 1953, when Wembley saw Matthews in his finest half-hour. McManaman does not score many goals – thirty-five in 190 full games at the start of 1996 – but he has an unusual knack of getting them in pairs. When I saw him at Chelsea in December 1995, smashing two tremendous eighteen-yard drives past Kharine, it was the eighth time he had collected two in a match. Not surprisingly, I wished he would hit more shots like that more often, for club and country.

Jamie Redknapp was born in the lovely little Hampshire seaside town of Barton-on-sea and started his football career at an even earlier age than both Fowler and McManaman, making his debut for Bournemouth as a substitute at Hull in January 1990, aged sixteen years and seven months. 'It was a bit soon, I suppose,' he says, 'but then I was a footballer's son and I probably knew a bit more about the game than others of my own age.' Redknapp senior, former West Ham winger Harry, was then Bournemouth's manager, and his assistant, who helped Jamie a lot in his time at Dean Court, was Jimmy Gabriel, that tough Everton wing-half of the 1960s. Gabriel later returned to Goodison to join the coaching staff there, and Redknapp junior followed him to Merseyside in January 1991, going to Anfield in return for £350,000, then a remarkable fee for a teenager. 'Naturally I didn't want to lose him,' says Harry Redknapp. 'But I knew that Jamie had a big future and he obviously had a better chance of success with a club like Liverpool.' At the time of the transfer, Redknapp the manager had only just recovered from injuries he received in a car crash that killed Bournemouth's former managing director and one-time player, Brian Tiler. And a fortnight after the deal was done, Redknapp junior had a traumatic experience of his own when his new boss,

Kenny Dalglish, decided to resign after the 4–4 FA Cup draw with Everton.

Not surprisingly, the lad took a while to settle into a new environment, but he worked at it, serving a typical apprenticeship in the reserves, then gradually establishing himself as a fixture. At twenty-three he has achieved quite a lot since he played in an under-11 league in Hampshire when only seven. He signed schoolboy forms for Tottenham but decided to join his dad's club, although Spurs got 25 per cent of the fee when Bournemouth sold him to Liverpool. He is a major figure in Liverpool's plans for the future, and seems sure to feature prominently in the England scheme, after injury pitched him out of the squad almost as soon as he had got into it. Before then he had appeared at youth under-17 and under-21 levels – quite a record. As a tall, tough, but constructive midfielder he has few superiors in the English game, although he has a tendency to drift out of the central sphere of action at times and, like McManaman, does not score as consistently as a player with his attributes might be expected to do. The most memorable of his goals so far arrived in the last minute of the last match of the 1994–5 season, when he scored from a free-kick to beat Blackburn 2–1, giving a spectacular finish to a pulsating game in which the fans hardly knew whether to cheer for the Reds or not. If Liverpool won, they might deprive Blackburn and Kenny Dalglish of the Premiership trophy; worst still, Manchester United might get it. The Redknapp goal ensured that Liverpool did win, but fortunately for the vast majority of

Anfielders, who dislike United with an intensity matched only by United's dislike of Liverpool, West Ham drew 1–1 against the Ferguson Fusiliers, thus preventing them from taking the title for a third season in succession. Four days earlier West Ham had assured themselves of another season of top-flight football by beating Liverpool 3–0. Harry Redknapp had taken over as manager at Upton Park, but his son did not do him any favours that night. Liverpool, as a team, were pretty ropey, but young Redknapp kept on battling, so much so that he got himself booked. What a professional!

Fowler, McManaman and Redknapp are young, fit role models, objects of fan-worship. How we envy them their success, and their youth. They could, collectively and individually, achieve a great deal, provided they keep their focus on the game. Fowler has had a couple of brushes with club officials and McManaman was involved in an unseemly on-field spat with Bruce Grobbelaar during one of his early appearances. Let us hope that the lessons have been learned and that they do not do anything to spoil their chances – and that they put aside their miserable showing in the 1996 FA Cup final. As for the other youngsters on the books, there is no obvious sign of newish burgeoning talent demanding an audience. Steve Harkness seemed to have settled on the left side of defence, before breaking a leg. Dominic Matteo (Scottish, would you believe) is very much a fringe player; Phil Charnock rather less than that. I am told that the likes of Lee Bryden, Iain

Brunskill and an Irish lad, Paul O'Donnell, have the makings, but obviously they have a long way to go yet.

The way ahead must involve more money being spent, irrespective of the implications of the Bosman judgment regarding transfers. Hopefully Mark Kennedy (£1.5m from Millwall) will prove to be a bargain at that sum, after an unlucky injury-affected start. Jason McAteer cost three times as much when he returned to his native Merseyside from Bolton last September, and he too needs to show himself to be a player out of the ordinary if he is to give value for the sum spent on him. And then there is Stan Collymore, the most expensive signing of all, and the most curious. A deadly finisher but a strange character. A defence-busting sprinter away from defenders, but far from revered at Palace, Southend and Forest. A player with a wonderful touch, yet too often not quite fit. Nobody could blame him for opting to live in countrified Cannock rather than metropolitan Merseyside, unless you thought of his salary (£12,000 a week, plus bonuses, advertising and so on) and wondered whether he should be just a bit more handily placed for training and matches. Nobody could blame him for his somewhat indiscreet admissions to *FourFourTwo* magazine (freedom of speech and all that), until you thought that perhaps others on the Anfield scene knew better than he did. And, with the best will in the world towards a young man, who was very much younger when he was deserted by his father, his pursuit of a percentage cut from that enormous fee, which he alleged Forest owed him because he had not asked for a transfer, was guaranteed to upset thousands on Merseywide and millions elsewhere, who can only wonder at the force driving otherwise sensible employers to involve themselves in such expense over such a pampered employee, no matter how good he might be at playing a game, no matter how the fans take to him.

A breakdown of the deal brings on a feeling of nausea. The transfer fee was apparently £8.5m. His wages and bonuses might be £700,000 a year. There might be the odd expenses, like hotel bills and petrol. And such an asset has to be insured. Collymore is now twenty-five. He may become a better player in his head, but he is unlikely to get any faster. He may now be at, or very close to, his peak; somehow I do not visualise his carrying on like a Rush or an Aldridge. Being generous, let us assume that Collymore spends ten years at Anfield and plays 400 games. That's a minimum of £7m in wages and bonuses, to add to the initial fee. Plus expenses. Say £16m, or £40,000 a game. For every game below 400, that average figure goes up. One argument I heard in Collymore's favour is the old chestnut about new players, especially record signings, putting hundreds or thousands on to the attendances, over the first few weeks at least. This used to be true, and still is in some places, but not at top clubs (including Liverpool) where the need for an all-seater ground has reduced the number of places available. Anfield's capacity is now about 41,000, and the average gate is pretty close to that. There simply is no room for Collymore, or anybody else, to pull in many more fans. I do not claim that the money spent on

Collymore will be wasted, in the end. But I am certain that a lot of it will be.

The reduced accommodation has been an expensive refinement. The provision of the Centenary Stand in 1992 and the rebuilding of the Kop two years later cost a total of £16m, which has had to be recouped through any channel possible. Liverpool have not gone down the Manchester United path of a new shirt for every month of the year and one for luck, but their off-field commercial activities are now light years away from the days (not all that long ago) when the only sales devices employed were a few advertisements in the programme. Now the club shop can take £30,000 on a match day, plus the mail order business, conference and banqueting facilities, the phone-in (the height, or depth, of banality), matchday magazine and museum. Television fees are enormous, making the pittance paid by the BBC for the old *Match of the Day* transmissions look even smaller. The first *Match of the Day* came from Anfield in 1964 (Hunt scored the first goal, against Arsenal) and the first colour *MOTD* show was from Anfield too, against West Ham five years later.

An FA Cup tie against Spurs in 1965 brought in Anfield's record receipts of £445,000, or approximately £11 a head – considerably cheaper than several other clubs would charge. For the 1995/6 season Liverpool had a premium rate of £13 or £16, depending on the site of the seat, for top matches; £12 and £15 for others. An adult/child combination can get in for £19.50 at a top game, £18.50 for the likes of Wimbledon. Season tickets account for about a third of the capacity and are incredibly cheap: £205 ordinary, £250 top whack. There are approximately 2,500 people on the waiting list which ranges from a year to three years, again depending on where the relevant seat is placed. The full-time staff at Anfield now number approximately 150, including cleaners, caterers, security (they used to have the surliest and least helpful members of the Corps of Commissionaires) and office workers. The office staff rarely get much credit, but they have worked very, very hard down the years, especially when the team have been doing well and playing a large number of matches. As an example of the 'unseen' part of their job, every Cup final has to be planned twice: once for the big day at Wembley, once for the replay. Every day the administration job includes tickets, transport, hotels, meals, media, foreign visitors, VIPs and dozens of other problems, including the frequent request for permission to scatter ashes on the pitch or around the ground. On match days or nights, the number of staff soars to 650, with stewards, gatemen, programme sellers and extra security drafted in. All this is the eventual responsibility of Peter Robinson, who joined the club as secretary in the 1960s and has since risen to be chief executive and a director. He was only the third secretary the club had had since the war, following Jack Rouse and Jimmy McInnes, a former player who committed suicide due to pressure of overwork. During my time spent following Liverpool affairs the directors have included several who have acted in FA and Football League capacities as well as working for the club, and a random list of those largely unsung but very valuable characters deserving mention comprises T V Williams, Billy McConnell, Sir John Smith, Harold Cartwright, Ronnie Williams, the Martindales (father and son), Eric Roberts and Cecil Hill. Plus Sid Reakes, whose high-speed driving ferried managers on many a hurried scouting mission. The present board, under chairman Moores, now includes Noel White, a member of the FA international committee with whom I am in agreement, in view of past and pending litigation, over the unsuitability of Terry Venables as England's surpremo.

The future for Liverpool remains bright, but not, in my view, burning bright. What they (and every other club) will do if and when the insatiable Murdoch tires of financing football and decides to patronise some other activity, God only knows. For the present, I can only hope that Liverpool find some more kids from their own doorstep to supplement all those big buys, and remember when the club's very name was enough to send gales of terror through opponents. In the new season, Liverpool will be able to go for the Cup Winners' Cup by default, after finishing runners-up to Manchester United in the FA Cup final last May. United, as double winners, naturally opt for the Champions Cup, leaving Liverpool to chase the only one of the six trophies available to English clubs that they have not held. I sincerely hope they get it, but I am not over-optimistic, despite the considerable amount of excellent soccer played, notably by Fowler and McManaman. This time, I hope there will be more emphasis on attack. Do you, like me, shudder at the memory of the return to Europe in 1995/6? Spartak Vladikavkaz were beaten in the away leg with goals from McManaman and Redknapp. At Anfield, with a one-goal advantage already established (and two away goals in the bank) against a team with no great pedigree and little experience of the game outside Russia, what did the team do? Put Fowler alone up front, pack midfield and the back, and slog out a goalless draw. In the next round they defended well against Brondby in Denmark to earn another 0–0 result, but at Anfield they again seemed reluctant to venture over the halfway line. Eventually, manager Evans took off two defenders and put on Collymore, who had recovered from injury, and Kennedy, to supplement Fowler and Rush. Too late: Brondby, a well-disciplined side with few pretensions to class, had snatched a goal, and held on to it. For the first time in their European history, going back thirty years of thrills and spills, laughter and tears, Liverpool had failed to score in three successive games.

Please, if only to honour the memory of all those who have gone before, let the future be more adventurous than that.

7

Appendix

Liverpool FC
Anfield Road, Liverpool L4 0TH
Tel 0151 263 2361
Year formed 1892
Turned professional 1892
Capacity 41,000
Nickname Reds or Pool

Club records

Attendance 61,905 v. Wolves, FA Cup 4th rd, 2 February 1952
Receipts £445,000 v. Spurs, FA Cup 6th rd, 11 March 1995
League victory 10–1 v. Rotherham Town, Div 2, 18 February 1896
Cup victory 11–0 v. Stromsgodset Drammen, Cup Winners' Cup 1st rd 1st leg, 17 September 1974
Defeat 1–9 v. Birmingham, Div 2, 11 December 1954
Most points (two for a win) 68, Div 1, 1978/9; (three for a win) 90, Div 1, 1987/8
Most League goals 106, Div 2, 1895/6

Highest League scorer in a season Roger Hunt, 41, Div 2, 1961/2
Most League goals in total Roger Hunt 245, 1959/69
Most capped player Ian Rush, 74, Wales
Most League appearances Ian Callaghan, 640, 1960–78
Record transfer fee received £2.75m from Juventus for Ian Rush, June 1986
Record transfer fee paid £8.5m to Nottingham Forest for Stan Collymore, June 1995

League record

Elected to Div 2 1893
1894 Promoted
1895 Relegated
1896 Promoted
1904 Relegated
1905 Promoted
1954 Relegated
1962 Promoted
1992 Premiership

Honours

Football League Division 1
Champions eighteen times (record) 1900/1, 1905/6, 1921/2, 1922/3, 1946/7, 1963/4, 1965/6, 1972/3, 1975/6, 1976/7, 1978/9, 1979/80, 1981/2, 1982/3, 1983/4, 1985/6, 1987/8, 1989/90
Second ten times

Football League Division 2
Champions four times 1893/4 (undefeated), 1895/6, 1904/5, 1961/2

LIVERPOOL

FA Cup
Winners five times 1965, 1974, 1986, 1989, 1992
Finalists six times 1914, 1950, 1971, 1977, 1988, 1996

League Cup
Winners five times (record) 1981, 1982, 1983, 1984, 1995
Finalists twice 1978, 1987

European Cup
Winners four times 1977, 1978, 1981, 1984
Finalists 1985

Cup Winners' Cup
Finalists 1966

Uefa Cup
Winners twice 1973, 1976

European Supercup
Winners 1977
Finalists twice 1978, 1985

World Club Championship
Finalists twice 1981, 1984

League Championships

Liverpool have won the First Division title a record eighteen times, and the Second Division four times. Their results in those twenty-two championship-winning seasons were:

	P	W	D	L	F	A	Pts
Div 2 1893/4	28	22	6	0	77	18	50
Div 2 1895/6	30	22	2	6	106	32	46
Div 1 1900/1	34	19	7	8	59	35	45
Div 2 1904/5	34	27	4	3	93	25	58
Div 1 1905/6	38	23	5	10	79	46	51

Div 1	1921/2	42	22	13	7	63	36	57
Div 1	1922/3	42	26	8	8	79	31	60
Div 1	1946/7	42	25	7	10	84	52	57
Div 2	1961/2	42	27	8	7	99	43	62
Div 1	1963/4	42	26	5	11	92	45	57
Div 1	1965/6	42	26	9	7	79	34	61
Div 1	1972/3	42	25	10	7	72	42	60
Div 1	1975/6	42	23	14	5	66	31	60
Div 1	1976/7	42	23	11	8	62	33	57
Div 1	1978/9	42	30	8	4	85	16	68+
Div 1	1979/80	42	25	10	7	81	30	60
Div 1	1981/2	42	26	9	7	80	32	87*
Div 1	1982/3	42	24	10	8	87	37	82
Div 1	1983/4	42	22	14	6	73	32	80
Div 1	1985/6	42	26	10	6	89	37	88
Div 1	1987/8	40	26	12	2	87	24	90++
Div 1	1989/90	38	23	10	5	78	37	79

+ record for any two-points-per-win season
* points for a win changed from two to three
++ equalled record for three-points-per-win season, since overtaken

FA Cup

Liverpool have won the FA Cup final five times and lost six times, scoring fifteen goals and conceding thirteen. The results and teams were:

1914 Burnley 0–1
Campbell, Longworth, Pursell, Fairfoul, Ferguson (capt), McKinlay, Sheldon, Metcalfe, Miller, Lacey, Nicholl

1950 Arsenal 0–2
Sidlow, Lambert, Spicer, Taylor (capt), L Hughes, W H Jones, Payne, Baron, Stubbins, Fagan, Liddell

LIVERPOOL

1965 Leeds 2–1 (aet)
Lawrence, Lawler, Byrne, Strong, Yeats (capt), Stevenson,
Callaghan, Hunt, St John, T Smith, Peter Thompson
Scorers: Hunt, St John

1971 Arsenal 1–2 (aet)
Clemence, Lawler, Lindsay, T Smith (capt), Lloyd, E
Hughes, Callaghan, A Evans (Peter Thompson), Heighway,
Toshack, Hall
Scorer: Heighway

1974 Newcastle 3–0
Clemence, T Smith, Lindsay, Phil Thompson, Cormack, E
Hughes (capt), Keegan, Hall, Heighway, Toshack, Callaghan
Scorers: Keegan 2, Heighway

1977 Manchester United 1–2
Clemence, Neal, J Jones, T Smith, R Kennedy, E Hughes
(capt), Keegan, Case, Heighway, McDermott, Johnson
(Callaghan)
Scorer: Case

1986 Everton 3–1
Grobbelaar, Lawrenson, Beglin, Nicol, Whelan, Hansen
(capt), Dalglish, Johnston, Rush, Molby, MacDonald
Scorers: Rush 2, Johnston

1988 Wimbledon 0–1
Grobbelaar, Gillespie, Ablett, Nicol, Spackman (Molby),
Hansen (capt), Beardsley, Aldridge (Johnston), Houghton,
Barnes, McMahon

1989 Everton 3–2 (aet)
Grobbelaar, Ablett, Staunton (Venison), Nicol, Whelan
(capt), Hansen, Beardsley, Aldridge (Rush), Houghton,
Barnes, McMahon
Scorers: Aldridge, Rush 2

1992 Sunderland 2–0

Grobbelaar, R Jones, Burrows, Nicol, Molby, Wright (capt),
Saunders, Houghton, Rush, Thomas, McManaman
Scorers: Thomas, Rush

1996 Manchester United 0–1

James, McAteer (Thomas), Wright, Scales, Babb,
McManaman, Redknapp, Barnes (capt), Fowler,
Collymore (Rush)
NB: Brackets denote substitutes

Most appearances: Callaghan, Grobbelaar, Nicol, Smith (4)
Most goals: Rush 5 (record for the competition), Keegan
2, Heighway 2

League Cup

Liverpool have won the League Cup, under its various titles,
a record five times and lost in two other finals, scoring
twelve goals and conceding eight in the ten matches. The
results and teams were:

**1978 League Cup: Nottingham Forest 0–1 (after 0–0
draw, aet)**

Clemence, T Smith, Neal, Phil Thompson, R Kennedy, E
Hughes (capt), Dalglish, Case, Heighway, McDermott,
Callaghan; Fairclough replaced Kennedy in the first match
and replaced Case in the second

1981 League Cup: West Ham 2–1 (after 1–1 draw, aet)

Clemence, Neal, A Kennedy, Irwin, R Kennedy, Hansen,
Dalglish, Lee, Heighway (Case), McDermott, Souness
(capt); in the replay Phil Thompson, Rush and Case
replaced Irwin, Heighway and Souness
Scorers: A Kennedy in the draw, then Dalglish and Hansen

1982 Milk Cup: Tottenham 3–1 (aet)
Grobbelaar, Neal, A Kennedy, Phil Thompson, Whelan,
Lawrenson, Dalglish, Lee, Rush, McDermott (Johnson),
Souness (capt)
Scorers: Whelan 2, Rush

1983 Milk Cup: Manchester United 2–1 (aet)
Grobbelaar, Neal, A Kennedy, Lawrenson, Whelan, Hansen,
Dalglish, Lee, Rush, Johnston (Fairclough), Souness
(capt)
Scorers: Kennedy, Whelan

1984 Milk Cup: Everton 1–0 (after 0–0 draw, aet)
Grobbelaar, Neal, A Kennedy, Lawrenson, Whelan, Hansen,
Dalglish, Lee, Rush, Johnston, Souness (capt); Robinson
replaced Johnston in the first match
Scorer: Souness

1987 Littlewoods Cup: Arsenal 1–2
Grobbelaar, Gillespie, Venison, Spackman, Whelan,
Hansen (capt), Walsh (Dalglish), Johnston, Rush, Molby,
McMahon (Wark)
Scorer: Rush

1995 Coca-Cola Cup: Bolton 2–1
James, R Jones, Scales, Ruddock, Babb, Bjornebye,
McManaman, Redknapp, Rush (capt), Fowler, Barnes
Scorer: McManaman 2

Most appearances: Dalglish and Neal (8), Rush (7), Hansen
and Alan Kennedy (6), McDermott, Phil Thompson and
Whelan (5)
Most goals: Whelan 3 (jointly the record for the
competition), Alan Kennedy, Rush and McManaman 2.

European Cup competitions

Liverpool have played in the finals of eight European competitions, involving ten matches of which they have won six (one of them on penalties), drawn one and lost three, scoring fourteen goals and conceding ten. The results and teams were:

1966 Cup Winners' Cup, Eintracht Frankfurt 1–2
Lawrence, Lawler, Byrne, Milne, Yeats (capt), Stevenson, Callaghan, Hunt, St John, T Smith, Peter Thompson
Scorer: Hunt

1973 Uefa Cup, Borussia Mönchengladbach, 3–0 (h), 0–2 (a)
First leg: Clemence, Lawler, Lindsay, T Smith, Lloyd, E Hughes (capt), Keegan, Cormack, Heighway (Hall), Toshack, Callaghan
Scorers: Keegan 2, Lloyd
Second leg: Unchanged (Boersma replaced Heighway)

1976 Uefa Cup, Bruges, 3–2 (h), 1–1 (a)
Clemence, T Smith, Neal, Phil Thompson, R Kennedy, E Hughes (capt), Keegan, Fairclough, Heighway, Toshack (Case), Callaghan
Scorers: R Kennedy, Case, Keegan (pen)
Second leg: Unchanged apart from Case for Fairclough, who substituted for Toshack
Scorer: Keegan

1977 Champions Cup, Borussia Mönchengladbach, Rome, 3–1
Clemence, Neal, J Jones, T Smith, R Kennedy, E Hughes (capt), Keegan, Case, Heighway, McDermott, Callaghan
Scorers: McDermott, Smith, Neal (pen)

1978 Champions Cup, Bruges, Wembley, 1–0
Clemence, Neal, Hansen, Phil Thompson, R Kennedy, Hughes (capt), Dalglish, Case (Heighway), Fairclough, McDermott, Souness
Scorer: Dalglish

1981 Champions Cup, Real Madrid, Paris, 1–0
Clemence, Neal, A Kennedy, Phil Thompson (capt), R Kennedy, Hansen, Dalglish (Case), Lee, Johnson, McDermott, Souness
Scorer: A Kennedy

1984 Champions Cup, Roma, Rome, 1–1 (aet); won 4–2 on penalties
Grobbelaar, Neal, A Kennedy, Lawrenson, Whelan, Hansen, Dalglish (Robinson), Lee, Rush, Johnston (Nicol), Souness (capt)
Scorer: Neal; shoot-out: Nicol (missed), Neal, Souness, Rush, A Kennedy

1986 Champions Cup, Juventus, Brussels, 0–1
Grobbelaar, Neal (capt), Beglin, Lawrenson (Gillespie), Nicol, Hansen, Dalglish, Whelan, Rush, Walsh (Johnston), Wark

Most appearances: Clemence and Neal 7, Callaghan, Hughes, Heighway and Smith 6, Keegan and Ray Kennedy 5
Most goals: Keegan 3, Alan Kennedy and Neal 2

The overall Cup final record in the various competitions is: played thirty-two, won sixteen (including one on penalties), drawn five and lost eleven, with forty-one goals scored and thirty-one conceded

Liverpool played in Europe from 1965 to 1985 inclusive –

twenty-one years in succession – before the Uefa ban following the Heysel disaster, and in 1991/2, 1992/3 and 1995/6.

They have appeared in the European Cup twelve times, the Cup Winners' Cup four times, and the Fairs/Uefa Cup eight times, playing 156 games and using 101 players.
They have lost only six home matches – against Leeds (Uefa Cup 1970/1, Red Star Belgrade (European Cup 1973/4), Ferencvaros (Cup Winners' Cup 1974/5), Genoa (Uefa Cup 1991/2), Spartak Moscow (Cup Winners' Cup 1992/3) and Brondby (Uefa Cup 1994/5).

	P	W	D	L	F	A	% won
Home	74	59	9	6	214	39	80
Away	74	28	17	29	81	78	38
Neutral	8	4	2	2	11	7	50
Total	156	91	28	37	306	124	58

NB Results are those at 90 or 120 minutes, disregarding away goals, toss of coin and shoot-outs

European appearances (incl. those as substitute):
88 Callaghan
84 Smith
77 Clemence
75 Hughes
69 Neal
66 Lawler
64 Heighway
47 Dalglish, Phil Thompson
46 Ray Kennedy
43 Peter Thompson, Hansen
40 Keegan
37 Grobbelaar, Rush
36 Yeats, Toshack, Souness
34 Hall, Alan Kennedy
33 Lawrence, Lee

32 St John
31 Hunt, Lloyd, Lindsay, McDermott, Case
27 Lawrenson
26 Stevenson
23 Whelan
22 Byrne
19 Boersma, Johnson, Nicol
18 Cormack
17 Johnston
16 Milne, Strong, Fairclough
15 Graham, McManaman
14 Marsh
13 Alun Evans
12 Joey Jones
11 Burrows, Wright
10 Harkness, Redknapp
 9 Wark
 8 McLaughlin, Walters, Rob Jones
 7 Ross, Robinson, Molby, Wright, Tanner
 6 Walsh, Ablett, Harkness, Redknapp
 5 Hateley, Irwin, Saunders, McMahon, James, Thomas,
   Barnes
 4 Moran, Hodgson, Houghton, Hooper, Rosenthal,
   Fowler, Babb
 3 Wall, Gillespie, MacDonald, Beglin, Venison, Hutchison
 2 Chisnall, Storton, Cohen, Stewart, Collymore,
   Ruddock, Scales
 1 Acourt, Wallace, Arrowsmith, Peplow, Roy Evans, Max
   Thompson, Livermore, Whitham, Kettle, Waddle,
   Money, Gayle, Barry Jones, Charnock, Mark Kennedy

The 306 European goals have been shared among fifty-
eight players plus four opponents:
20 Rush
17 Hunt

12 Keegan, Case, R Kennedy, McDermott
11 Lawler, Heighway, Neal
10 St John, Callaghan, Toshack, Dalglish
 9 Hughes, Saunders
 8 Smith, Boersma, Johnson
 7 Alun Evans, Souness
 6 Peter Thompson, Whelan
 5 Graham, Wark
 4 Lindsay, Fairclough, Lee, Phil Thompson, own goal
 3 Hateley, Alan Kennedy, Hansen, Walsh
 2 Wallace, Yeats, Strong, Cormack, Hall, Lawrenson,
    Johnston, Nicol, Robinson, Houghton, Stewart,
    McManaman
 1 Chisnall, Byrne, Stevenson, Lloyd, Ross, Hodgson,
    Beglin, Molby, Walters, Marsh, Venison, Wright,
    Hutchison, Redknapp

Liverpool have played opponents from twenty-nine countries:
Austria, Belgium, Bulgaria, Cyprus, Denmark, England, East
Germany, Finland, France, Greece, Hungary, Holland, Ice-
land, Italy, Luxembourg, Northern Ireland, Norway, Poland,
Portugal, Republic of Ireland, Romania, Scotland, Spain,
Sweden, Switzerland, Turkey, USSR, West Germany and
Yugoslavia.

Seventeen clubs have knocked Liverpool out of Europe, but
Ferencvaros of Hungary are the only club to do so twice.
The clubs to beat them are:
Inter Milan, Juventus and Genoa (Italy); Borussia Dortmund
and Bayern Munich (Germany); Ajax (Holland); Ferencvaros
(Hungary, twice); Atletico Bilbao (Spain); Vitoria Setubal
(Portugal); Leeds and Nottingham Forest (England); Red Star
Belgrade (Yugoslavia); Dinamo Tbilisi and Spartak Moscow

(USSR); CSKA Sofia (Bulgaria); Widzew Lodz (Poland); and Brondby (Denmark)

World Club Cup

Liverpool have played in two games for this incorrectly named trophy, which is now sponsored by Toyota and staged in Tokyo between the European Champions Cup holders and their South American club equivalent, holders of the Libertadores Cup. Clubs from Africa, Asia and Oceania do not compete. In 1981 Liverpool lost 0–3 to Flamengo of Brazil, and in 1984 they were beaten 0–1 by Independiente of Argentina.

European Super Cup

Liverpool have contested this trophy, a play-off between the winners of the Champions Cup and the Cup Winners' Cup, on three occasions, involving five matches. In 1971 they drew 1–1 in Hamburg and won the home leg 6–0. In 1978 they lost 1–3 to Anderlecht in Brussels and won 2–1 at home. In 1985 they lost 0–2 to Juventus in Turin.

Most appearances: Neal 5, Dalglish, Hughes and R Kennedy 4
Most goals: Fairclough 3, McDermott 3

Charity Shield

Liverpool have played in the Charity Shield eighteen times, winning seven and losing five, scoring twenty goals and conceding seventeen:

1922   Huddersfield 0–1
1964   West Ham 2–2

1965   Manchester United 2–2
1966   Everton 1–0
1972   Leicester 0–1
1974   Leeds 1–1, won 6–5 on penalties
1976   Southampton 1–0
1977   Manchester United 0–0
1979   Arsenal 3–1
1980   West Ham 1–0
1982   Tottenham 1–0
1983   Manchester United 0–2
1984   Everton 0–1
1986   Everton 1–1
1988   Wimbledon 2–0
1989   Arsenal 1–0
1990   Manchester United 1–1
1992   Leeds 3–4

Most appearances: Grobbelaar 8, Hansen, Neal, Rush and Whelan 7

Most goals: Rush and McDermott 3

Liverpool Cup defeats by teams in a lower division:
1902   1–4 at Southampton (Southern League) FA 2nd
1903   1–2 at Man United (2nd) FA 1st
1909   2–3 h to Norwich (SL) FA 2nd
1912   0–3 at Fulham (2nd) FA 2nd
1920   1–2 at Huddersfield (2nd) FA 4th
1925   0–1 at Southampton (2nd) FA 4th
1926   1–3 at Fulham (2nd) FA 4th
1930   1–2 h to Cardiff (2nd) FA 3rd
1934   0–3 h to Bolton (2nd) FA 5th
1937   0–3 at Norwich (2nd) FA 3rd
1947   0–1 to Burnley (2nd) FA SF
1951   1–3 at Norwich (3rd South) FA 3rd
1953   0–1 at Gateshead (3rd North) FA 3rd
1957   1–2 at Southend (3rd South) FA 3rd*

1959   1–2 at Worcester (SL) FA 3rd*
1964   1–2 h to Swansea (2nd) FA 6th
1968   2–3 at Bolton (2nd) LC 2nd rd replay
1970   0–1 at Watford (2nd) FA 6th
1971   0–2 at Swindon (2nd) LC 3rd
1979   0–1 at Sheffield Utd (2nd) LC 2nd
1980   0–1 at Bradford C (4th) LC 2nd (won second leg 4–0)
1984   0–2 at Brighton (2nd) FA 4th
1992   0–1 at Peterborough (3rd) LC 4th
1993   0–2 h to Bolton (1st) FA 3rd replay**
1994   0–1 h to Bristol C (1st) FA 3rd replay**

* Liverpool in Div 2
** Liverpool in Premiership

When Liverpool drew 4–4 at home to Chesterfield in September 1992, in the Rumbelows Cup, after being 0–2 and 1–3 down, it was the first time since their 1–5 defeat by Derby in 1898 that they had conceded so many goals in a home cup game.

Liverpool did not lose a home FA Cup tie between the 0–1 to Huddersfield in the fifth round, 1938, and 0–2 to the same club at the same stage in 1955. They had won all sixteen home ties in between.

Between losing to Leicester in the fifth round in 1969 and to Brighton at the same stage in 1983, Liverpool played twenty-five FA Cup games at Anfield, winning eighteen and drawing seven.

Liverpool did not lose any of eighty-five home matches between 21 January 1978 (2–3 to Birmingham) and 31 January 1981 (1–2 to Leicester, then bottom of the table). In that time they played sixty-three First Division games, nine League Cup ties, seven games in Europe and six FA Cup matches, winning sixty-nine and drawing sixteen, with 212 goals scored and thirty-six conceded.

Between a 0–2 defeat by Leeds on 1 January 1972 and a 1–1 draw with Derby on 20 January 1973, they won twenty-one successive home League games.

The club's longest spell without a victory spanned fourteen matches in the relegation season, between 12 December 1953 and 3 April 1954, and comprised nine defeats and five draws.

They did not win a home League fixture between 13 October 1951 and 22 March 1952, their results in that period being 2–5, 1–1, 0–0, 2–2, 1–1, 1–1, 1–1, 1–2, 1–1, 1–1. In the same period they won four away games and drew three.

Their total of nineteen draws out of forty-two matches that season was a record for the First Division.

Eight Liverpool players have been chosen as Footballer of the Year by the Football Writers Association – Ian Callaghan 1974, Kevin Keegan 1976, Emlyn Hughes 1977, Kenny Dalglish 1979 and 1983, Terry McDermott 1980, Ian Rush 1984, John Barnes 1988 and 1990, and Steve Nicol 1989. The journalists gave a special award to the Liverpool players for the compassion shown to bereaved families after the Hillsborough disaster in 1989. The Player of the Year award voted for by members of the Professional Footballers Association went to McDermott in 1980, Dalglish in 1983, Rush in 1984 and Barnes in 1988. Rush (1983) and Robbie Fowler (1995 and 1996) have won the PFA Young Player of the Year award.

The Manager of the Year award went to Bill Shankly in 1973, to Bob Paisley in 1976, 1977, 1979, 1980, 1982 and 1983, to Joe Fagan in 1984, and to Kenny Dalglish in 1986, 1988 and 1990. (Dalglish also won it in 1995 as manager of Blackburn.) The PFA Merit award was given to Shankly in 1978 and Paisley in 1983.

The last amateur to play in Liverpool's senior side was South African goalkeeper Doug Rudham, who made twenty-five appearances in 1954/5 and then turned professional, playing another forty-one games.

During the 1954/5 season Liverpool had a run of eight games in which they conceded a total of ten penalties, all but one of them resulting in goals.

Transfers

The following sixteen players have cost Liverpool £1m or more:

1995	Stan Collymore	Nottingham Forest	£8.5m
1996	Jason McAteer	Bolton	£4.2m
1994	Phil Babb	Coventry	£3.6m
1994	John Scales	Wimbledon	£3.5m
1991	Dean Saunders	Derby	£2.9m
1988	Ian Rush	Juventus	£2.8m
1993	Neil Ruddock	Tottenham	£2.5m
1992	Paul Stewart	Tottenham	£2.3m
1993	Nigel Clough	Nottingham Forest	£2.3m
1991	Mark Wright	Derby	£2.2m
1987	Peter Beardsley	Newcastle	£1.9m
1991	Michael Thomas	Arsenal	£1.5m
1993	Julian Dicks	West Ham	£1.5m
1995	Mark Kennedy	Millwall	£1.5m
1991	Mark Walters	Rangers	£1.5m
1992	David James	Watford	£1.2m

In addition, signings during the past decade of John Aldridge, John Barnes, Stig Bjornebye, David Burrows, Jimmy Carter, Gary Gillespie, Steve Harkness, Ray Houghton, Glenn Hysen, Rob Jones, Istvan Kozma, Steve McMahon, Torben

Piechnik, Jamie Redknapp, Ronny Rosenthal, Barry Venison and Paul Walsh added up to several millions more. Earlier major signings included Kenny Dalglish from Celtic in 1977 for £440,000 and Graeme Souness from Middlesbrough in 1978 for £352,000, and in 1968 Alun Evans had become Britain's first £100,000 teenager when he joined Liverpool from Wolves.

The following sales have brought Liverpool £1m or more:

1987	Ian Rush	Juventus	£3.3m
1991	Dean Saunders	Aston Villa	£2.3m
1994	Don Hutchison	West Ham	£1.5m
1996	Nigel Clough	Man City	£1.2m
1989	John Aldridge	Real Sociedad	£1.1m
1991	Steve Staunton	Aston Villa	£1.1m
1991	Peter Beardsley	Everton	£1m

Attendances

Liverpool averaged more than 44,000 spectators per home League game in each of the first four seasons after World War Two, and following their return to the First Division in 1962 they averaged more than 41,000 for eighteen success-ive seasons, including a club record 48,103 in 1972/3. The various ground improvements since then have led to a drop in capacity.

The highest attendance at Anfield, 61,905, was at an FA Cup tie against Wolves in 1952. The highest League gate was 58,757 against Chelsea in 1949, and the highest in the Premiership stands at 44,619 against Everton in 1993.

There were several four-figure gates in the club's earlier years: the lowest attendance for a competitive match since the war was 9,092 for a League Cup game against Brentford in 1983, and the lowest in the League was 11,976 against Scunthorpe in 1959.